Cliffs

ON STE

THE GRAPES OF WRATH

by Kelly McGrath Vlcek

In This Book!

- Get the author background and literary context you need to fully understand the book

- Learn the important traits and motivations of all the major characters

- Know what happens *and* what it means with detailed Summary & Analysis

- Deepen your knowledge with Critical Essays covering key aspects of the book

- Check your understanding with study help and review questions

LEARNEO

CliffsNotes® On Steinbeck's *The Grapes of Wrath*
Published by:
Learneo, Inc.
2000 Seaport Blvd., Third Floor
Redwood City, CA 94063
www.learneo.com

Copyright © 2022 Learneo, Inc., Redwood City, CA
Cataloging-in-Publication information is available from the Library of Congress.
ISBN-13: 979-8-88915-950-6

No part of this publication may be reproduced, stored in a retrieval system, or transmitted in any form or by any means, electronic, mechanical, photocopying, recording, or otherwise, without written permission of the publisher or authorization through payment of the appropriate per-copy fee. For information regarding permissions, write to Learneo, Inc., Attention: Legal Department, 2000 Seaport Blvd., Third Floor, Redwood City, California, 94063, or email legal@coursehero.com.

LIMIT OF LIABILITY/DISClAIMER OF WARRANTY: THE PUBLISHER AND AUTHOR HAVE USED THEIR BEST EFFORTS IN PREPARING THIS BOOK. THE PUBLISHER AND AUTHOR MAKE NO REPRESENTATIONS OR WARRANTIES WITH RESPECT TO THE ACCURACY OR COMPLETENESS OF THE CONTENTS OF THIS BOOK AND SPECIFICALLY DISCLAIM ANY IMPLIED WARRANTIES OF MERCHANTABILITY OR FITNESS FOR A PARTICULAR PURPOSE. THERE ARE NO WARRANTIES WHICH EXTEND BEYOND THE DESCRIPTIONS CONTAINED IN THIS PARAGRAPH. NO WARRANTY MAY BE CREATED OR EXTENDED BY SALES REPRESENTATIVES OR WRITTEN SALES MATERIALS. THE ACCURACY AND COMPLETENESS OF THE INFORMATION PROVIDED HEREIN AND THE OPINIONS STATED HEREIN ARE NOT GUARANTEED OR WARRANTED TO PRODUCE ANY PARTICULAR RESULTS, AND THE ADVICE AND STRATEGIES CONTAINED HEREIN MAY NOT BE SUITABLE FOR EVERY IND MD UAL. NEITHER THE PUBLISHER NOR AUTHOR SHALL BE LIABLE FOR ANY WSS OF PROFIT OR ANY OTHER COMMERCIAL DAMAGES, INCLUDING BUT NOT LIMITED TO SPECIAL, INCIDENTAL, CONSEQUENTIAL, OR OTHER DAMAGES. FULFILLMENT OF EACH COUPON OFFER IS THE RESPONSIBILITY OF THE OFFEROR.

Trademarks: Cliffs, CliffsNotes, CliffsNotes on Literature, CliffsAP, CliffsComplete, Cliffs Test Prep, Cliffs Quick Review, CliffsNote-a-Day, and all other related trademarks, logos, and trade dresses are trademarked (or registered trademarked) by Learneo, Inc., in the United States and other countries—and therefore, may not be used without written permission. All other trademarks mentioned are property of their respective owners. Learneo, Inc. is not associated with any product or vendor mentioned in this book.

Table of Contents

INTRODUCTION AND CONTEXT 1
   The Grapes of Wrath at a Glance 2
   Book Summary 4
   About *The Grapes of Wrath* 6
   Character List 10
   Character Map 12
   John Steinbeck Biography 13

SUMMARY AND ANALYSIS 17
   Chapter 1 18
   Chapter 2 21
   Chapter 3 24
   Chapter 4 26
   Chapter 5 29
   Chapter 6 32
   Chapter 7 35
   Chapter 8 37
   Chapter 9 40
   Chapter 10 42
   Chapter 11 45
   Chapter 12 47
   Chapter 13 48
   Chapter 14 51
   Chapter 15 53
   Chapter 16 56
   Chapter 17 59
   Chapter 18 61
   Chapter 19 64
   Chapter 20 67
   Chapter 21 70
   Chapter 22 72
   Chapter 23 74
   Chapter 24 76
   Chapter 25 79
   Chapter 26 81
   Chapter 27 84
   Chapter 28 86
   Chapter 29 89
   Chapter 30 91

CHARACTER ANALYSIS 94
- Tom Joad 95
- Ma Joad 95
- Jim Casy 96
- Rose of Sharon Joad 97
- Pa Joad 97
- Other Characters 98

CRITICAL ESSAYS 101
- Use of Literary Devices in the Intercalary Chapters of *The Grapes of Wrath* 102
- Philosophical Influences on Steinbeck's Social Theory 104

STUDY HELP 106
- Quiz 107
- Full Glossary for *The Grapes of Wrath* 110
- Essay Questions 119
- Practice Projects 120

INTRODUCTION AND CONTEXT

The Grapes of Wrath at a Glance

John Steinbeck's *The Grapes of Wrath*, Tom Joad and his family are forced from their farm in the Depression-era Oklahoma Dust Bowl and set out for California along with thousands of others in search of jobs, land, and hope for a brighter future. Considered John Steinbeck's masterpiece, *The Grapes of Wrath* is a story of human unity and love as well as the need for cooperative rather than individualistic ideals during hard times.

Written by: John Steinbeck

Type of Work: novel

Genres: historical fiction

First Published: 1939

Setting: the Great Depression; Oklahoma

Main Characters: Tom Joad; Ma Joad; Jim Casy; Rose of Sharon Joad; Pa Joad

Major Thematic Topics: love; strength in unity; re-birth; survival

Motifs: disrupted power structures

Major Symbols: turtle crossing the road; vacant houses; Ma Joad; the truck

The three most important aspects of *The Grapes of Wrath:*

- *The Grapes of Wrath* takes place during America's Great Depression, which lasted from the Stock Market Crash of October 1929 until World War II began 12 years later. During this time, a long period of drought and high winds affected large parts of the American Midwest, including much of the state of Oklahoma, creating what was called the Dust Bowl. Many of the people in the lower Midwest moved elsewhere, hoping to find fertile land on which to make a living.
- Tom Joad is the protagonist, or main character, of *The Grapes of Wrath*. Tom is the book's hero as well despite the fact that Tom attacks a policeman at one point in the novel and beats a man at another point, becoming a cave-dwelling fugitive as a result. Tom's actions, although illegal according to the letter of the law, are morally just.
- The most famous image in *The Grapes of Wrath* is the novel's final one, in which Rose of Sharon Joad, whose baby was recently stillborn, breast-feeds a sickly, starving man on the floor of an old barn. In this image, Steinbeck powerfully dramatizes the desperate plight of Depression-era migrant workers, whom the author felt had been abandoned by society.

Book Summary

In Depression-era Oklahoma, Tom Joad hitchhikes home after being paroled from the state penitentiary. Along the road, he encounters Jim Casy, a preacher Tom remembers from childhood. Casy explains that he is no longer a preacher, having lost his calling. He still believes in the Holy Spirit, but not necessarily the spirituality mandated by organized religion. For Casy, the Holy Spirit is love. Not just the love of God or Jesus, but the love of all humans. He maintains that all people are holy, everyone being part of the whole soul of humankind. Tom invites Casy to join him on his walk home.

When they arrive at what was once the Joad farm, Tom and Casy find it abandoned. Muley Graves, a Joad neighbor, approaches and tells Tom that his family has been tractored off their land by the bank. They have moved in with his Uncle John and are preparing to leave for California to find work. Tom and Casy spend the night near the deserted farm and head to Uncle John's early the next morning.

The family is preparing for their journey to California when Tom and Casy arrive. Casy asks whether he can journey west with the Joads. The Joads agree to take him along. Once their belongings have been sold, everyone except Granpa is anxious to get started. They pack the truck, but Granpa has decided he wants to stay on the land, and they must drug Granpa in order to get him in the truck. They are on the highway by dawn.

The family stops that first evening next to a migrant couple whose car has broken down. The Wilsons are gracious, offering their tent to Granpa who has a stroke and dies. Tom and Al fix the Wilson's car, and the two families decide to travel together.

In New Mexico, the Wilson's touring car breaks down again, and the families are forced to stop. Granma has become increasingly ill since Granpa's death, and Tom suggests the others take the truck and continue on. Ma refuses to go, insisting that the family stay together. She picks up the jack handle to support her point, and the rest of the family gives in. As they reach the desert bordering California, Sairy Wilson becomes so ill that she is unable to continue. The Joads leave the Wilsons and continue across the California desert on their own.

Granma's health continues to deteriorate, and as the truck starts its nighttime trek across the desert, Ma knows that Granma will not survive. Knowing that they cannot afford to stop, Ma lies in the back of the truck with Granma. Midway across the desert, Granma dies. By dawn, the Joads have climbed out of the desert and stop the truck to gaze down upon the beautiful Bakersfield valley. Ma tells them that Granma has passed. She must be buried a pauper because the family does not have enough money to bury her.

The Joads stop at the first camp they come to, a dirty Hooverville of tents and makeshift shelters. The men are talking to Floyd Knowles, a young man in the camp, when a businessman accompanied by a cop offers them work. When Floyd asks for a wage offer in writing, he is accused of being a "red," and the cop attempts to arrest him. Tom trips the cop, and Casy kicks him. When the cop regains consciousness, Casy gives himself up to the law in order to divert attention away from Tom. The Joads immediately leave to avoid any further trouble.

The Joads travel south to a government-run camp in Weedpatch. Here, the community governs itself, electing committees to deal with clean-up, discipline, and entertainment. The Joads are comfortable but, after a month, are still unable to find any work and realize they must move on.

They are offered work picking peaches in Tulare. The camp gate is surrounded by a large group of men shouting and waving. The Joads, escorted through the gate by state police, begin work immediately. They are paid five cents a box, not sufficient to feed the family a day's meal. After the first day of picking, Tom wanders outside the ranch. He meets up with Jim Casy, who is leading a strike against the peach orchard owners who want to pay two-and-a-half cents a box. Tom learns his family is being paid five cents because they are working as strikebreakers. As the men talk, authorities sneak up, looking for Casy, the presumed leader of the strike. Unprovoked, one of the men strikes Casy on the head, killing him. Without thinking, Tom begins beating Casy's killer. The other men intervene, and Tom's nose is broken. He escapes, hiding in the peach orchard until he can reach his house.

Marked by his scarred face and broken nose, Tom becomes a fugitive, hidden by his family. The Joads flee the peach ranch at the first daylight. They find work picking cotton and share an empty boxcar with another family, the Wainwrights. Tom hides in a nearby cave where his mother leaves him food. The family is comfortable for a time, earning enough to eat meat daily. One day, however, young Ruthie gets in a fight with another child. She threatens to call her big brother who is hiding because he has killed two men. Ma rushes to tell Tom he must leave for his own safety. Tom agrees and leaves with plans to carry on the social work that Jim Casy has begun.

Al gets engaged to sixteen-year-old Agnes Wainwright. As the cotton picking slows, the rains come. It rains steadily, and the water levels begin to rise. The night that Rose of Sharon goes into labor, the river threatens to flood the boxcar. Pa, Uncle John, Al and the rest of the men try to build an embankment to contain the river, but are unsuccessful. Rose of Sharon's baby is stillborn.

After a few days, the rain subsides. Leaving Al and the Wainwrights, the remaining Joads abandon the boxcar for higher ground. They find shelter in an old barn already occupied by a boy and his starving father. The child tells the Joads that his father has not eaten in six days and is unable to keep down solid food. Rose of Sharon offers him the breast milk no longer needed for her own child. The others leave the barn as she cradles the dying man to her breast.

About *The Grapes of Wrath*

Introduction
Steinbeck's background and previous writing experience found him well prepared to tackle the chronicle of the dispossessed Joads as they search for work in Depression-era California. Much of Steinbeck's young adult life was spent around the ranches of California's Salinas Valley. Working as a ranchhand, he gained firsthand knowledge of the migrant laborers who worked the farms. From this experience grew an awareness of the social inequalities affecting the labor force. With the publication of *In Dubious Battle,* Steinbeck established his reputation as a social critic and champion of the migrant worker. Recognizing his new status as a social commentator, *The San Francisco News* commissioned him to write a series of articles about conditions in the migrant worker's camps in California's Central Valley. This work, along with the time spent traveling cross-country with an Oklahoman migrant family, provided Steinbeck with the bulk of the episodic material needed to write *The Grapes of Wrath.*

Historical Background
The plot of Steinbeck's masterpiece is rooted in the historical and social events of 1930s America, specifically the environmental disaster coined the Dust Bowl by an Oklahoma reporter in 1935. Drought had been a serious problem for the Great Plains region of the United States for many decades prior to the 1930s. In the late 1880s, the land began to be settled by sharecroppers for agricultural purposes, but a particularly severe drought in 1894 brought such widespread crop destruction that, in some areas, as many as 90 percent of the settlers abandoned their claims. During this drought period came several reports of dust clouds covering the land, suffocating livestock and impeding visibility. In the early twentieth century, greater rainfall and the replacement of bare fields with sod helped restore the agricultural productivity of the Plains states, and by World War I, large-scale farming had begun again. Soon after the war, however, the weather began to warm, and again, drought became a chronic condition of the area. Meanwhile, poor farming techniques of numerous sharecroppers had decimated the agricultural capacity of the land, the harsh cotton crops robbing soil of its nutrients. These two conditions combined to make it difficult for farmers to bring in a profitable crop.

With the stock market crash of 1929 and the subsequent decline in the U.S. economy, banks became desperate for a way to recoup losses. Maintaining that it was more lucrative to merge the sharecroppers' holdings into one large farm to be cultivated by a corporation, land companies began removing families from their farms. Most sharecroppers had been so unsuccessful that the banks already owned their property. Uneducated and inexperienced in non-agrarian matters, the dispossessed families were ill equipped for other employment.

Naïve and adrift, the migrants were in the perfect position to be taken advantage of by the propaganda techniques of the large farm owners. Hundreds of thousands of handbills were distributed throughout the stricken land, promising bountiful opportunities for farm workers at good wages. These pamphlets targeted the sharecroppers' desire for land and respectability, enticing them westward with the lure of financial stability. With few other options available to them, the farmers loaded their families and their most precious belongings on battered automobiles and headed to California.

The legions of homeless families emigrating to California became something of a phenomenon. Previously, farm labor in California had been primarily the province of *habitual* migrant workers, mostly single men who followed the seasons and crops as a chosen way of life. The economic conditions of the 1930s had created a second type of migrant worker, the *removal* migrant. These dispossessed agricultural workers were forced into a nomadic existence and longed only to find a place to rest and settle. More than 450,000 people would eventually be forced to take to the road in search of employment. These desperate migrant families frightened the established citizens of California and were labeled *Okies,* a derogatory term referring to any outcast from the Southwest or northern plain states.

Critical Reception of The Grapes of Wrath

From its first printing, *The Grapes of Wrath* enjoyed immediate and widespread commercial success. Advanced sales of the novel shot it onto the national bestseller list where it was to stay throughout 1939 and 1940. Although mass circulation reviewers complained of its unconventional structure and downcast ending, the novel garnered a number of awards, including a Pulitzer Prize.

However, not everyone was convinced of the novel's brilliance. The book was attacked vehemently in both California and Oklahoma, labeled in one magazine editorial as communist propaganda. In Kern County, California, the Board of Supervisors banned *The Grapes of Wrath* in both schools and libraries. *The San Bernardino Sun* said, "the fallacy of this [story] should not be dignified by a denial." Most of the negative energy in Oklahoma was targeted at discrediting Steinbeck's portrayal of the state and its inhabitants. An article in *The Oklahoma City Times,* titled "Grapes of Wrath? Obscenity and Inaccuracy," was typical of the reaction in that state. In retrospect, it is probable that many people were ashamed by both the terrible dilemma of the migrant families and the inhumane treatment they received from society. Much like the German citizens who refused to believe in the existence of the Nazi death camps, a denial of the truth of the social situation could be viewed as an attempt to lessen their own culpability.

In the years that followed, *The Grapes of Wrath* experienced a shift in critical reception. The passage of time had distanced the book from the volatile social and historical circumstances of its setting, allowing readers a clearer perspective of Steinbeck's work. At the time of its first appearance in 1939, the novel was considered, at best, an influential social tract, and at worst, full-fledged propaganda. Following World War II, it became clear that if the novel were going to maintain its influential status, it would have to be considered not only for its social philosophies, but also for its artistic merits. Although some insisted the novel was no more than a romantic "wagons west" saga, many respected literary critics began to seriously examine the literary elements of the novel. For the next three decades, indeed up to today, critics have delved into the work's artistic and conceptual traits, scrutinizing and debating its use of biblical allusions and symbolism, the effectiveness of its unconventional narrative structure, and the validity of its ending. The wealth of criticism that has emerged proves *The Grapes of Wrath* is indeed one of the most important works in American literature, and, for the perceptive reader, provides an abundance of artistic and philosophical considerations.

The Structure of The Grapes of Wrath

From its initial publication, the unconventional structure of *The Grapes of Wrath* has been both attacked and misunderstood by a great number of readers. Steinbeck's method of inserting chapters of general information or commentary between straightforward narrative chapters frustrates many readers who consider them distracting, an interruption in the "real" story of the Joad family.

These *intercalary* chapters, as they were termed by critic Peter Lisca, serve a distinct purpose in commenting on and expanding the events of the narrative proper. Sixteen intercalary chapters are included in the book, accounting for approximately 100 pages, or one-sixth of the text. Although the Joad characters do not appear in any of these intercalary chapters, many of the incidents found in these chapters foreshadow similar situations experienced by the Joads. Some, written in a variety of literary styles, provide a generalized, dramatic overview of the central social conditions affecting the main characters, while others provide historical information and direct commentary on book's social and political background.

Steinbeck uses recurring symbols, motifs, and specific narrative episodes to link each intercalary chapter with its adjacent narrative counterparts so that the intercalary chapters, far from being an intrusion, actually unify and strengthen the dominant themes of the novel. The land turtle of the brilliantly descriptive and symbolic Chapter 3 will be picked up by Tom Joad in Chapter 4, and the dramatic monologue of a used car salesman figures immediately before the Joads' purchase of a truck for their journey west. Likewise, the Joads' search for work in California is preceded by a history of migrant labor in that state.

Steinbeck knew the importance of his readers grasping the greater social message presented in *The Grapes of Wrath*. The suffering of the wandering families and their oppression by larger, more powerful forces was a social crisis of widespread magnitude. He was concerned that readers would not comprehend this urgent, yet impersonal problem unless they could focus their sympathy on the ordeals of a specific family. At the same time, however, he did not want the struggles of the Joads to be considered isolated events, specific only to a particular family. The use of intercalary chapters provides a balance, allowing Steinbeck to realize the ultimate artistic goal: To weave together specific social facts and lyrical elements to create a personal story that expresses universal truths about the human condition.

Steinbeck's Social Philosophy

The social philosophy presented by Steinbeck in *The Grapes of Wrath* is complex and somewhat contradictory. The basic social theory expressed by Jim Casy, acted on by Ma Joad, and eventually realized by Tom Joad, is one that compels the so-called "little people," the impoverished and dispossessed, to come together in order to gain power against capital-minded owners. This social philosophy maintains that human survival is dependent upon the banding together of humans to find strength in group unity and action. The elaboration of this theory in the novel is seen in the education of the oppressed and disadvantaged with the organization of unions and strikes as vehicles of group protest and change.

Theoretically, Steinbeck's philosophy appears to be based upon the socialist theories of Lenin and Marx, although it shows the clear influence of several distinctly American philosophies. The Emersonian concept of the Oversoul is expressed in the earthy folk language of Jim Casy, who believes that all person's souls are really just part of one big soul. The symbolic contrasts between the vitality of the land and the "deadness" of inanimate machines represent the theory of Jeffersonian agrarianism, which holds that the identification of humankind with soil is necessary for the continuation of the life cycle. The pragmatism of Henry James, in which the meaning and truth of all concepts are defined by their practical consequences, is seen in the active approach of Ma and Tom to adversity. Finally, in Casy's assertion that "maybe it's all men an' all women we love," we find the idea of humanism, a love of all persons and the embracing of mass democracy found in the works of Walt Whitman and Carl Sandburg.

Character List

Tom Joad The novel's main character and second Joad son. As the novel opens, he is returning to his family after his parole from the McAlester State Penitentiary. Among the novel's characters, Tom shows the most growth in his realization of the concept of human unity and love.

Jim Casy A former preacher. Concerned with his controversial beliefs about what is sinful and what is holy, he has renounced his calling. Traveling to California with the Joads, he plans to listen to the people and help them. Casy is the spokesman for the author's main theories, including the multi-faceted themes of love and strength in unity.

Ma Joad Wife and mother. Ma is the backbone of the Joad family: strong-minded and resolute. Her main concern is that the family unit not be broken. She is the physical embodiment of Steinbeck's theory of love.

Pa Joad Patriarch of the Joad clan. Pa is a sharecropper whose land has just been foreclosed on by the bank. Somewhat lost and weakened, he leads his family to California in search of work.

Rose of Sharon Eldest Joad daughter. Rose of Sharon is pregnant and married to 19-year-old Connie Rivers. Self-absorbed by her pregnancy, she has many plans and dreams for their life in California. At the novel's close, she represents life-giving force.

Granma and Granpa The couple who first began farming on the land that Pa has lost.

Noah Joad The oldest Joad son. Noah is slow-moving and emotionally distant, perhaps the result of an unintentional injury caused by Pa during Noah's birth.

Al Joad Sixteen-year-old Joad son. Al willingly admits that only cars and girls interest him. He is responsible for the maintenance of the family's truck during the journey to California.

Ruthie Joad The youngest Joad daughter. Ruthie is 12 years old and caught between childishness and adolescence.

Winfield Joad The youngest Joad family member. Winfield is 10 years old.

Muley Graves A Joad neighbor in Oklahoma. Muley has also been tractored off his land. He chooses to stay behind when his family leaves for California, an illustration of the effect of loss on those who have been driven from their land.

Ivy and Sarah (Sairy) Wilson Traveling companions of the Joads. A couple from Kansas, the Wilsons meet the Joads when their touring car breaks down. After Al and Tom fix their car, they travel with the family to the California border. The cooperation between the Wilsons and the Joads exemplifies the strength that is found in persons helping others.

Mr. and Mrs. Wainwright The Wainwrights share a boxcar with the Joads at the end of the novel. Like the Wilsons, their union with the Joads underscores the novel's theme of human unity.

Agnes Wainwright The Wainwright's 16-year-old daughter. She is engaged to Al Joad at the end of the novel.

Ezra Huston Chairman of the central committee in the government camp at Weedpatch.

Willie Eaton Texan in charge of the entertainment committee at the government camp. He and his committee members thwart a staged riot attempt by the Farmers Association.

Character Map

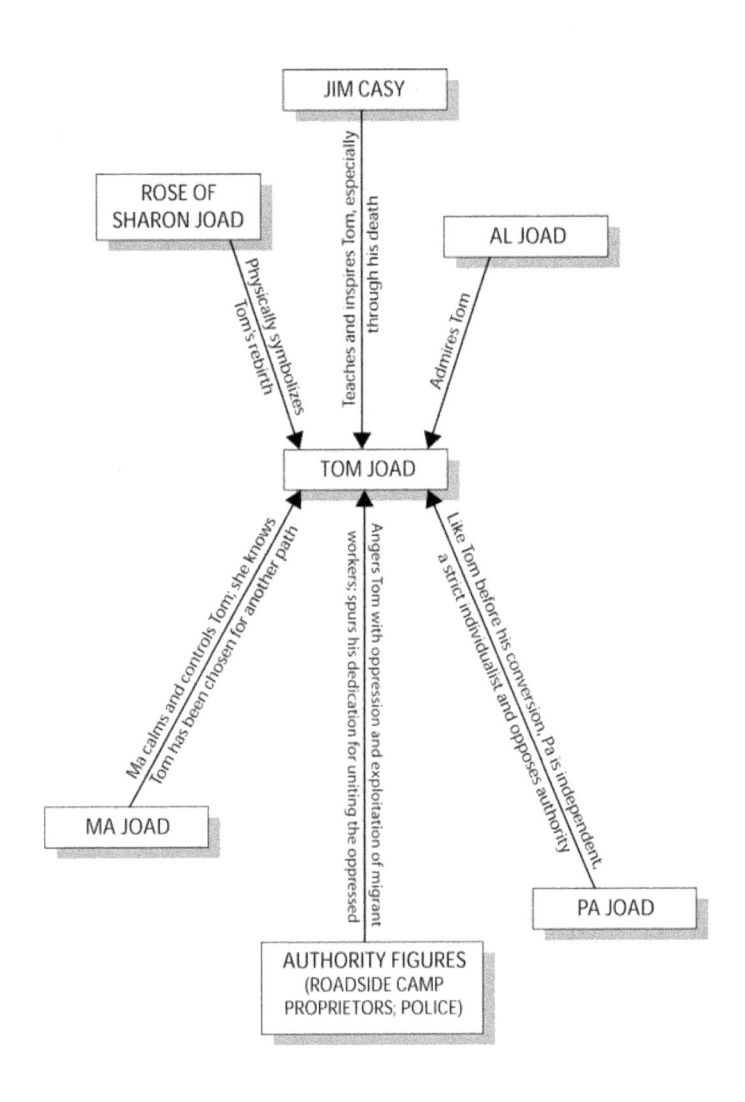

- **JIM CASY** — Teaches and inspires Tom, especially through his death
- **ROSE OF SHARON JOAD** — Physically symbolizes Tom's rebirth
- **AL JOAD** — Admires Tom
- **MA JOAD** — Ma calms and controls Tom; she knows Tom has been chosen for another path
- **AUTHORITY FIGURES (ROADSIDE CAMP PROPRIETORS; POLICE)** — Angers Tom with oppression and exploitation of migrant workers; spurs his dedication for uniting the oppressed
- **PA JOAD** — Like Tom before his conversion, Pa is independent, a strict individualist and opposes authority

All arrows point to **TOM JOAD**.

John Steinbeck Biography

Family and Education

John Steinbeck was a man of experience first and words second. He lived passionately and observed both shrewdly and humanely, focusing on human struggles with the forces of nature around him and the passions within him. Using as its backdrop the tremendous beauty and epic power of the California land he knew so well, Steinbeck's writing strove to make meaning out of the hardships he saw.

From his earliest memory, John Steinbeck wanted to be a serious writer. He was born on February 27, 1902, to a middle-class family in Salinas, California. His father, John Ernst, Sr., was a well-to-do miller and local politician, and his mother, Olivia Hamilton, taught school. Under his mother's influence, Steinbeck read widely and was influenced by many great authors: Eliot, Dostoevsky, Hardy, and most notably, Malory. Malory's *Morte d'Arthur*, given to Steinbeck on his ninth birthday, took him away from his own middle-class existence and showed him the power of the theme of good versus evil. While Malory had a great influence on Steinbeck's writing style, Steinbeck described the syntactical rhythms and sweeping epic scope of the King James Bible as having the most lasting impression on his work.

Never a scholar, Steinbeck spent a large part of his youth outdoors, working and playing in the Salinas Valley, midway up the California coast. This lush, fertile, and often harsh land would become the backdrop for his most enduring works. Although stifled by academic discipline, Steinbeck loved to write, publishing pieces in his high school paper, and later, in the student paper at Stanford University. Steinbeck's studies at the university often took a back seat to more active pursuits: he worked on ranches, in factories, did construction work, and was even a member of a road-building gang. Although he came from a strongly middle-class background, Steinbeck's experiences as a laborer provided him with the first-hand observations that would fuel so much of his writing. After five years of intermittent studies, he left Stanford without a degree.

Early Work

In 1925, Steinbeck traveled to New York in an attempt to make a living as a writer. The city was not welcoming, however, and when it was suggested that he try writing advertising copy to break into the industry, Steinbeck said farewell. He completed a set of short stories, which was rejected by publishers, and returned to California.

While working as a lodge caretaker in the Sierra Mountains, Steinbeck completed his first novel, a historical swashbuckler entitled *Cup of Gold*. However, success continued to elude the young writer. With monumental bad timing, his first novel was published in late 1929, just two months before the stock market crash changed the atmosphere of the entire country. According to Lewis Gannett, about 1,500 copies of the book were sold, but it was not taken seriously by the few critics who reviewed it.

Shortly after the publication of *Cup of Gold,* Steinbeck eloped with a local girl named Carol Henning, and with his father's help, they set up home in the small community of Pacific Grove. Here Steinbeck met Ed Ricketts, the man who was to have the greatest influence on both his life and his work. Ricketts, the proprietor of a marine specimen supply house on the outskirts of Pacific Grove, proved a perfect companion for Steinbeck: Both men loved to drink, think, and discuss life philosophies. Together they would develop a non-teological philosophy (focusing on the world as it *is,* not as it *should* or *might* be) that would figure prominently in the pragmatism of many of the main characters in *The Grapes of Wrath.* Ricketts would later be immortalized as "Doc" in *Cannery Row.*

Steinbeck's first, and arguably best, novel to be set in California was published in 1932. Unfortunately, the Depression was in full swing, and the first two publishing houses that handled *The Pastures of Heaven* went broke before the novel could be bound. In 1933, the author published *To A God Unknown,* an unsuccessful allegory, and sold the first two parts of his short story, "The Red Pony."

His first national recognition came when "The Murder" won the O. Henry Prize for short stories in 1934, and was cemented the following year with the strong commercial reception of *Tortilla Flat.* The publication of this light-hearted tale about vagabonds on the Monterey peninsula marked the beginning of his association with Pascal Covici, the man who was to publish the rest of Steinbeck's major works. The critical reviews were mixed, but the novel proved popular enough with the reading public that Steinbeck was able to sell the movie rights for $3,000, a sum of money greater than any he had received before.

After a trip to Mexico with Ed Ricketts and a change of residence to Los Gatos, a suburb of San Jose, Steinbeck settled down to write *In Dubious Battle,* a powerful study of a labor strike, which stirred up considerable critical controversy. The year 1936 proved to be a busy one for Steinbeck. Not only did he publish *In Dubious Battle,* he finished several short stories and was commissioned to write a series of articles for *The San Francisco News* about conditions in California migrant worker camps. These articles were published in October 1936, and later gathered together in a pamphlet entitled "Their Blood Was Strong." Steinbeck's experiences with these migrant workers would be the foundation on which he based *The Grapes of Wrath.*

Career Highlights

Steinbeck became a celebrity with the publication of *Of Mice and Men* in 1937. The novel was well received both critically and popularly. Chosen as a Book-of-the-Month-Club selection, *Of Mice and Men* soon became a national bestseller. Steinbeck returned to New York in triumph and toured Europe. He eventually settled in the fashionable East Coast writers' colony of Buck's County, where he worked on the script of the play version of the novel with the famous playwright, George Kaufman. The play opened in late November 1937 to rave reviews, received the New York

Drama Critic Circle's Award for Best Play, and enjoyed a long, successful run before being made into a theatrical film. Even Steinbeck's good fortune, however, could not save his publishing house from ruin. Pascal Covici would leave the financially defunct firm of Covici, Friede to become the executive editor of Viking Press, and Steinbeck would follow. In 1938, Viking published *The Long Valley*, a collection of Steinbeck's short stories.

Although enjoying huge success both financially and critically, Steinbeck remained a man of the people. He refused an offer from *Life* magazine to write about the migrant workers because he felt it would be wrong to make money off their misfortune. He continued to base his writing on actual experiences, living and working among the very folks he would use as material for his work. In fact, on the night that *Of Mice and Men* opened on Broadway, he was in a squatters camp with a group of migrants with whom he had traveled from Oklahoma.

The Grapes of Wrath was published in 1939 and immediately caused a literary furor, well documented by Warren French. The top selling novel of 1939, it won the Pulitzer Prize and the American Booksellers Award, merits which supported Steinbeck's election to membership in the National Institute of Arts and Letters. A movie version of the novel was soon filmed and also received critical accolades. Although there are not specific financial records documenting the sale of the book, the numerous American printings and foreign translations would attest to a generous increase in Steinbeck's income. This likelihood is supported by the fact that his first wife, suing for divorce in 1942, received a $220,000 settlement.

In the years immediately following *The Grapes of Wrath*, Steinbeck, now somewhat of a literary celebrity, traveled and toiled primarily on war-related works. He and his best friend, Ed Ricketts, returned to Mexico twice. The first trip, in March 1940, is chronicled in *The Sea of Cortez;* the men returned the next month to film the semi-documentary film, *The Forgotten Village*. The work would occupy him for the remainder of the year. In 1942, he wrote an Army Air Force-commissioned book entitled *Bombs Away,* and donated the earnings of his play-novelette, *The Moon Is Down,* to the war effort.

Perhaps as an antidote to the suffering he had seen in the war, Steinbeck published *Cannery Row* in 1945, a light-hearted romanticizing of the pre-war antics of the vagabonds and idlers of Monterey's Cannery Row. He followed in 1947 with what many consider his finest short story, "The Pearl," and the novel *The Wayward Bus*. The year 1948 marked several important events in Steinbeck's life. He was elected into the American Academy of Arts and Letters and divorced from his second wife, Gwyn Verdon. Perhaps the most traumatic event of the year was the loss of his closest friend, Ed Ricketts, in an automobile accident. In 1950, Steinbeck married Elaine Scott. His third marriage seemed to invigorate him, and he began work on a new novel, an ambitious epic of good and evil set in his own Salinas Valley. *East of Eden* was published in 1952 to lukewarm critical reception. Steinbeck's output during the

1950s slowed, consisting mainly of magazine pieces and an unsuccessful rehashing of *Cannery Row* entitled *Sweet Thursday*. In 1961, Steinbeck re-emerged with *The Winter of Our Discontent,* and in 1962, he was awarded the world's highest literary recognition, a Nobel Prize for literature. Not content to settle down comfortably, Steinbeck took to the road in late 1961, armed with a stack of maps and an elderly poodle named Charlie. His adventures across the country were recounted in one of his last works, *Travels with Charlie*. John Steinbeck died on December 20, 1968.

SUMMARY AND ANALYSIS

Chapter 1

Summary

After early May, no more rain came to the red and gray country of Oklahoma. Soon the earth crusted and clouds of dust surrounded all moving objects. Midway through June, a few storm clouds teased the country but dropped very little rain. The wind became stronger and soon the dust hung in the air like fog. People were forced to tie handkerchiefs over their faces and wear goggles over their eyes.

When the wind stopped, the men and women came out to survey the damage to the fields. Everyone, even the children, was subdued. They were waiting for the reaction of the men, to see whether they would break. The men did not break, but began figuring how to deal with the ruined corn. The women resumed their housework and the children their play, for they knew as long as the men were okay, the family would be fine.

Analysis

Chapter 1 establishes the epic context and tone for the entire novel. This brief, but important, opening chapter provides a backdrop for the main events of the narrative, describing the event primarily responsible for spurring the great migration to California during the 1930s. The destructive force of the Dust Bowl is staggeringly described as a backward life cycle, a regression from fertile green to a dead and dusty brown. The deterioration of the land that forces the farmers to huddle and "figger" foreshadows the plight of the Joads: Forced off their land by a bank looking for profit, they will move west seeking a new livelihood. The beautifully apocalyptic description of the slow spread of decay throughout the Oklahoma country is strongly influenced by the King James Bible and sets the brooding and oppressive tone of the novel.

The opening chapter also introduces many of the themes that will be played out throughout the course of the novel. The suggestion of unity and human dignity in the huddled circle of men will be developed in the narrative. Likewise, the theme of survival, particularly survival in the face of environmental destruction, is implied by the refusal of the men to break. This theme, too, will be examined in detail in the narrative chapters.

Chapter 1 is the first of the so-called intercalary chapters, inserted between the narrative chapters, which are generalized accounts of the social, economic, and historical situations that shape the events of the novel. These chapters provide significant commentary on the narrative elements of the novel and establish that this story is not one of an isolated group of individuals. The Joads' troubles — dispossessed, stripped of dignity, and struggling to maintain familial unity — are not unique to their family, but representative of an entire population of migrating people. Throughout the novel, the broad events of these intercalary chapters will be brought into sharp, personalized focus by the specific plight of the Joad family.

Glossary

perplexity the condition of being perplexed; bewilderment; confusion.

hams a) the backs of the thighs; b) the thighs and buttocks together.

Chapter 2

Summary
A well-kept transport truck is stopped outside a roadside diner. Tom Joad, freshly paroled from McAlester Penitentiary, walks down the road and pauses by the diner. Clad in new, cheaply made clothing, he sits down on the truck's running board to loosen his new shoes. When the driver walks out to his truck, Tom asks for a ride. The driver refuses at first, citing the NO RIDERS sign, but Tom suggests that sometimes "a guy'll be a good guy even if some rich bastard makes him carry a sticker." The driver wants to be a good guy so he agrees to give him a ride, telling him to crouch down on the running board until they are out of sight of the diner.

Once on the road, the driver immediately begins sizing up his passenger. When he learns that Tom's father is a cropper on 40 acres, he shares his surprise that they "ain't been tractored out." Tom becomes irritated at the driver's meddling questions until they reach Tom's road. Getting out of the truck, he discloses that he has been prison for homicide, sentenced for seven years but out in four for good behavior.

Analysis
The second chapter sets the central plot in motion, provides basic background information, and foreshadows events that will come. The main character of Tom Joad is introduced, and his basic characteristics are established. As Tom will undergo the greatest personal change in the novel, it is important to note his individualism and quick temper. His irritation at the nosiness of the truck driver underscores his independent and somewhat solitary nature. In the course of the conversation between Tom and the truck driver, many key facts are furnished. For example, the Joads' current living situation is foreshadowed by the driver's surprised reaction to Tom's statement that his family are sharecroppers, "They ain't been tractored out yet?" Tom's admission to the truck driver that he has been in prison reveals an important fact, his position as a parolee, which will prove critical to his departure at the end of the novel.

The author also lays the groundwork for a basic theme in his work: the constant tension between those who have and those who have not. This conflict is brought up when Tom forces the truck driver to decide whose side he is on — that of the worker or that of the owners. This particular conflict will be passionately addressed in the intercalary chapters that examine the roots of the changing social structures present specifically in California.

The setting of the roadside diner will be revisited in Chapter 15. In both chapters, the diner serves as a point of human convergence: the migrant families, the wealthy travelers in their sleek, insulated cars, the truck drivers who cover the roads in the service of higher powers, and the stationary cooks and waitresses all connect in this setting. In the trucker's lament of the loneliness on the road, we begin to hear minor notes of Steinbeck's message of human unity. It is for human company, not food, that truckers stop at the highway diners. Later in the novel, we will see that the migrants are also looking for a human bond at the truck stops — they are armed with the simple faith that there might be someone inside willing to help them out.

Glossary

cat slang for Caterpillar: trademark for a tractor equipped on each side with a continuous roller belt over cogged wheels, for moving over rough or muddy ground.

chambray a smooth fabric of cotton, made by weaving white or unbleached threads across a colored warp: used for dresses, shirts, and so on.

hobnailed describing boots or heavy shoes with short, broad-headed nails in the soles.

dogs slang term for feet.

croppers sharecroppers.

truck skinner a skinner is a mule driver; here refers to a truck driver.

McAlester State Penitentiary near McAlester, Oklahoma.

Chapter 3

Summary
A land turtle navigates through a dry patch of ground toward a slanted highway embankment full of oat beards and foxtails. Resolute and unswerving, the turtle fights its way up the slope to the highway and begins to cross the hot pavement. A speeding car swerves onto the shoulder to avoid the turtle. Moments later, a truck purposefully clips the shell of the turtle, sending it spinning to the side of the highway, landing on its back. Eventually, the turtle rights itself, crawls down the embankment, and continues on its way.

Analysis
Whenever an entire chapter is devoted to the movement of a seemingly inconsequential creature, a reader should take note. Chapter 3, with its stunningly realistic depiction of an old turtle gamely trying to cross the highway, can (and should) be read as symbolic of the Joads and their struggle. Like the turtle, the Joads are victimized by the hostile environment in which they exist, yet, also like the turtle, they persist in their journey. This journey takes the turtle southwest, the same direction that the Joads will be traveling. The author follows the turtle in painstaking detail, beginning with its arduous climb up the embankment and through its ordeal on the highway, where it is humanely avoided by one driver, only to be purposefully attacked by a second. Because of its protective shell, however, this collision with the truck only hastens the turtle to the other side of the highway, its original destination.

In the course of its travels, the turtle unwittingly carries an oat beard, a symbol of new life, in its shell. This oat beard is carried to the other side of the highway, where it falls out and is covered with dirt by the turtle's dragging shell, ready to produce again. With this symbol, Steinbeck specifically refers to the notion that humanity and its life force will continue to regenerate regardless of obstacles and setbacks. Steinbeck will revisit this theme of re-birth in Chapter 14 when he claims that humankind is defined by its need to struggle toward goals that grow beyond work, "having stepped forward, he may slip back, but only half a step, never the full step back." This concept will also be supported later in the novel with Ma Joad's assertion that "we're the people that live we're the people — we go on."

Glossary

foxtails plants with cylindrical spikes bearing spikelets interspersed with stiff bristles.

head of wild oats the uppermost part of a plant's foliage.

oat beard a hairy outgrowth on the head of certain grains and grasses.

Chapter 4

Summary

As the truck returns to the highway, Tom walks down the road toward his family's farm. The hot sun beats down on him, so he takes off his shoes and wraps them in his coat. Spying the horned turtle from the previous chapter, he picks it up and wraps it in the coat as well. Continuing down the road, he sees a man lying under the tree, singing to Jesus. Tom recognizes him as the preacher, Jim Casy, but Casy is quick to tell him that he has been filled with sinful thoughts and is no longer a preacher.

Bothered by his need to have sex with a young girl after a meeting, Casy has been wandering about, trying to figure out how men can be "sinful" when they are full of the Holy Spirit. He has lost faith in organized religion, finally deciding that what it's really all about is love: not love of Jesus or God, but love of all men. He has come to the conclusion that no one has an individual soul, but that everyone's soul is a part of a larger soul that includes all people. With thoughts like these, he feels he should no longer be a preacher. Tom agrees, and Casy decides to walk to the Joad farm with Tom. When they reach the Joad place, it is deserted, and Tom realizes that something is wrong.

Analysis

Of critical importance to the novel, Chapter 4 provides the first strand of a social philosophy advocated by Steinbeck: an evocation of the Emersonian concept of the Oversoul. This idea is delivered by the character of Jim Casy, who is believed to be the carrier of Steinbeck's philosophical beliefs. When we first meet Casy, we learn that his ideas of religion and spirituality have changed. Troubled by his own sensuality, and wrestling with the concept of sin and virtue, he has "gone off on his own to give her a damn good thinkin' about." When he returns, he has experienced a re-birth, a re-consideration of the Holy Spirit and what it means to be holy. Casy has decided that sin and virtue are all part of the same thing. The souls of all humans are only small parts of a larger soul that encompasses everyone — the Oversoul. All that really matters is love of all men and all women, and the Holy Spirit is, in fact, the human spirit. Humans are what Casy loves, not this person he does not know named Jesus. He is turning from an abstract concept to a more personalized form of religion based on the actions of individuals.

The structure of the novel shows the general plight of the "Okies" by focusing on the specific problems of a single family. Connections are constantly maintained between the general, or intercalary, chapters and the narrative chapters. In this case, Tom picks up the turtle from the previous chapter. This correlation between the abstract and the specific is also characterized by the contrast between Jim Casy and Tom Joad. Casy deals with the theoretical, concerned with defining the problems that are facing humanity. Although he has abandoned a religion of general ideals, it isn't until much later in the novel that he physically supports his beliefs through action. Tom, on the other hand, is a man of action, although his motivation is primarily self-centered. He is concerned with himself and his own family, but eventually grows because of his intuitive response to people in need. In the end, abstract thoughts are not what matter as much as the actions of individuals.

Glossary

meetin' an assembly or place of assembly for worship.

prodigal here refers to the wastrel son in biblical scripture who was welcomed back warmly on his homecoming in repentance (Luke 15:11-32).

Chapter 5

Summary

Representatives of the company come to tell the tenants that they must get off the land. Sharecropping is no longer profitable, so the bank has bought the land to farm. The men representing the company are mean or nice or cold because they are ashamed of what they are doing, yet none take responsibility for their actions. It is not their fault, but the fault of the Bank, and the Bank is not a person. The squatters try to bargain, offering to rotate crops or to take a smaller share, but the bank men are not interested. The tenants argue that the land belongs to them because their families have lived and died on it, but the bank men only reply, "I'm sorry."

The next day, a tractor arrives, bulldozing whatever is in its path. Disconnected from the land on which he works, the driver is not a living man, but an extension of the tractor. The tenants recognize him as the son of a neighbor and question why he would help to put his neighbors out of their homes. He replies that he has his own family to take care of, and the bank will pay him three dollars a day, every day. The tenant wants to know whom he should kill to get his land back, but there is no person he can fight. While the tenant tries to figure out what to do, the tractor bites into the corner of his house.

Analysis

In keeping with the nature of the intercalary chapters, the conflict revealed in this chapter is general, not involving individuals, but groups of people representative of socio-economic classes. By looking at the larger picture, the widespread effects of the drought and the bank foreclosures are emphasized: It is not just the Joads, but a great number of families who will be forced off their land. The abstract conflict between the Bank/owner and the tenant, first witnessed in the novel's second chapter, begins to develop here. Steinbeck begins to draw a clear line between the sympathetic farmer who shares stories of his family's connection to the land and the company, an impersonal conglomerate that is isolated from attack. The generalizations of the action become specific in the next chapter when the Joads are actually forced off their land.

A second component of Steinbeck's social philosophy, related to the theory of Jeffersonian agrarianism, is examined in the portrayal of the tenants' connection with the land, as well as the resultant destruction that occurs when he is torn from it. These men take their dignity and self-respect from their proximity to earth and its cycles of growth. When this relationship is severed, they lose their identity and begin to drift, both figuratively and literally. Their trauma is underscored by the tenant's observation, "Funny thing how it is. If a man owns a little property, that property is him, it's part of him, and it's like him." This theme will be played out continuously throughout the novel, most notably in Granpa's death and, later, in the starvation of the migrants when they are denied a patch of land on which to raise food.

Steinbeck's sharp contrast between the humanness of the farmer and the inhumanness of the banks and their machines reinforces this notion of the loss that occurs when people are removed from the life force of land. The Bank is a monster which paradoxically lives off profits, not the produce of the earth. The tractor, a mechanized symbol of a new way of life, is not alive, but nonetheless eats homes as it furrows the repossessed farms. Deterred by nothing, the tractor destroys all human elements in its path. When the driver climbs on the tractor, he becomes linked to its goal of gaining individual profit. His perception and protest effectively "goggled" and "muzzled," he refuses to consider the plight of the neighbors he is tractoring off the land. The tractor driver prioritizes the feeding his own family over the economic tragedy of his fellow farmers. His contribution to the economic decline of his community is in contrast to Casy's theory that all must help each other because they are all part of the same being.

Glossary

tenant a person who farms land owned by another and pays rent in cash or in a share of the crops.

harrows frames with spikes or sharp-edged disks, drawn by a horse or tractor and used for breaking up and leveling plowed ground, covering seeds, rooting up weeds, and so on.

diesel a type of internal-combustion engine that burns fuel oil.

spam trademark for a kind of canned luncheon meat made from pieces of seasoned pork and ham pressed into a loaf.

side-meat meat from the side of a pig; specifically, bacon or salt pork.

Chapter 6

Summary

Tom and Casy see that the Joad house has been pushed off its foundations. They check to see whether a note has been left for Tom, but only find clear evidence that the house has been deserted. The house has not been rummaged or looted, an indication that something is wrong throughout the neighborhood. With the family gone, Tom unwraps the turtle and puts him on the ground. The turtle continues in the same direction he was going when Tom picked him up.

Tom recognizes his neighbor, Muley Graves, approaching. Muley tells "Tommy" that the family has been tractored off their land. They are temporarily staying with Uncle John until they can earn enough money to go to California. Tom and Casy learn that Muley's family has already left for California, but he was emotionally unable to leave the land where he had grown up. Casy admonishes Muley for breaking up the family.

Muley shares his supper of cooked rabbit, while telling them how out of touch he's become from living alone. Listening to Muley helps Casy recognize his calling: he needs to go out on the road to give comfort to these dispossessed people. Tom, meanwhile, realizes that he will be breaking his parole if he leaves the state with his family.

An approaching car's headlights illuminate the field, and the three men hide at Muley's warning that they would now be considered trespassers. Muley takes Tom and Casy to a small cave to hide for the night, but Tom chooses to sleep outdoors. They plan to move on to Uncle John's in the morning.

Analysis

In Chapter 6, the generalized actions of the previous chapter are made concrete. The young tractor driver now has a name, Willy Feeley, and just as the tenant's house is knocked off its foundation at the end of the last chapter, so now the Joad house is found crumpled at the corner. The threat of the faceless farmer to use his gun is materialized in Muley's news that Granpa actually shot out a tractor's headlights. Muley Graves' statement, "Place where folks live is them folks. They ain't whole, out lonely on the road. They ain't alive no more," not only reiterates the plea of the tenant in Chapter 5, it points out the moral deterioration that is a parallel result of economic decline.

Muley physically reinforces Casy's theory of love: All persons are a part of the same spirit, and a refusal to unite together effectively disassociates an individual from the whole. In contrast to the betrayal of the tractor driver in the last chapter, who will feed his own children while others go hungry, Muley finds that he must share his meal. "I ain't got no choice if a fella's got somepin to eat an' another fella's hungry — why, the first fella ain't got no choice." An individual's very existence is defined by his responsibility (or lack of responsibility) for those with whom he interacts. Muley intuitively realizes this, although he struggles to express it. Ma will recall this line of thinking in Chapter 8 with her willingness to feed strangers.

The reappearance of the turtle serves to unify the narrative and intercalary chapters. Released from the confines of Tom's jacket, it continues in its original southwest direction, the same way the Joads will travel, thus reinforcing its symbolic nature. Unlike the purposeful turtle, however, the Joads are forced onto the road, unsure of their destination or their future.

Tom's refusal to hide in the cave at the close of the chapter should be noted as it foreshadows the events at the end of the novel. At this point in the novel, Tom does not understand the concept of strength in group unity that Casy is struggling to articulate. He is concerned primarily for himself. Not until he is forced to hide in a cave does Tom complete his moral conversion.

Glossary

two-by-four any length of lumber two inches thick and four inches wide when untrimmed.

boil an inflamed, painful, pus-filled swelling on the skin, caused by localized infection.

lifer [slang] a person sentenced to imprisonment for life.

Chapter 7

Summary
The disadvantaged farmers face even bleaker prospects as they attempt to sell their household goods and buy vehicles to carry them westward. Fast-talking salesmen, looking to capitalize on the tenants' desperation and naiveté, sell them barely-running jalopies at hugely inflated prices. The salesmen pour sawdust into the engine to cover up noises, and they disguise balding tires. The tenants realize they're being taken advantage of, but unfortunately, have no other choice than to take what is offered.

Analysis
This intercalary chapter is a staccato monologue delivered by a used car salesman pitching jalopies to dispossessed croppers. Steinbeck's literary technique is similar to the newsreel style popularized by his American contemporary, John Dos Passos. The rhythm suggests the franticness of the situation, a situation in which the salesman has complete control. With the speed and confidence of his words, the salesman is able to fluster and manipulate the stricken farmers, and the repetition of his spiel draws attention to the fact that this was an oft-repeated scenario. Again, this general situation will be specifically realized by the Joads — they need to purchase a car for their trek to California and are exploited by sales tactics they don't understand.

Glossary

jalopy [slang] an old, ramshackle automobile.

lemon [slang] something, especially a manufactured article, that is defective or imperfect.

carrying charges the costs associated with property ownership, as taxes, upkeep, and so on.

Chapter 8

Summary

Casy and Tom leave for Uncle John's house at daybreak. While walking, Tom describes Uncle John to Casy, coloring him as a lonely, somewhat touched older man. As Tom and Casy approach John's property, they see the family preparing for their trip west. Tom surprises Pa as he works on the truck. Pa's first concern is that "Tommy" has broken out. Assured that he is on parole, Pa decides they should surprise Ma who is preparing breakfast.

Ma is overjoyed to see Tom, but instantly worried that prison has made him "mean" and full of hate. He reassures her that it has not, and after searching his eyes, she can see that he is telling the truth. Tom is angry that they have been forced from their home, but Ma cautions him that he can't fight the bank alone. She figures that if everybody got mad together, they couldn't be put down, but everyone seems lost and dazed. Adrift and directionless, they are unable to band together to fight with a common purpose.

Tom is reunited with more family members at breakfast. Granpa and Granma are excited to see Tom. Behind them is Noah, the eldest son, who is quiet and slow. At Granma's insistence, Casy says grace over the meal, although he explains he is no longer a preacher. In his prayer, he says that holiness is when all people are working together, not focused on their individual desires. Tom asks after the rest of the family members and learns that his younger brother, Al, is out chasing girls, and Rose of Sharon, his younger sister, is now married to a neighboring boy, Connie Rivers. She is in the early stages of her first pregnancy. The two youngest Joads, 10-year-old Winfield and 12-year-old Ruthie, have gone to Sallisaw with Uncle John to sell a load of household belongings. Once everything has been sold, they will have about $150 for the trip. Within a day or two, the family plans to leave for the west.

Analysis

Ma's character is critical to both Tom's growth and the reader's understanding of the idea of humanism, the third component of Steinbeck's social philosophy. Her most obvious purpose in the novel is to provide the physical expression of Jim Casy's ideals. Her actions consistently emphasize the theory of love and spirit haltingly defined by the preacher, that love and unity among men is necessary if people are to survive. For Ma, this unity begins with her family. Her relief at seeing Tom stems primarily from her fear that they would have to leave the state with the family broken. Ma also unknowingly expresses the pragmatic aspect of the social theory that Casy is struggling to understand. The preacher yearns to bring a practical spiritual help to those folks who are suffering, but doesn't know how. He spends his time thinking, wondering how to express this principle of love, while Ma immediately acts upon it. She is a pragmatist, focusing not on what might or should be, but how life is.

Although Pa is the "head" of the family, Ma is its backbone: It is her strength and support that keeps the family functioning. She knows each member's weaknesses and is accepting of them. Her ability to calm Tom enables him to evolve spiritually. Understanding his reckless temper and independent nature, she is frightened that in jail he has become "mean." She holds his face and scans his eyes, searching for truth that may not be expressed in words. This action foreshadows a later event in the novel in which she must hold Tom's face in the dark in order to "see" him.

For the majority of the novel's action, Ma works desperately to keep her family intact, not realizing that survival depends on embracing all persons as family. Her love operates on a deeper level, however, a level that indicates she seems to intuitively understand Casy's message that all people are holy and deserving of love because they all belong to one greater soul. Ma is always the first in the family to offer comfort and nourishment to others, just one indication of her subconscious, unconditional love. The larger concept of this love, that survival will only be possible through group action is glimpsed only fleetingly in her plea to Tom, "I got to dreamin'. If we was all mad the same way, Tommy — they wouldn't hunt nobody down." She stops, not comprehending the validity of her dream.

Glossary

hackles the hairs on a dog's neck and back that bristle, as when the dog is ready to fight.

meerschaum a soft, claylike, heat-resistant mineral used for tobacco pipes.

Mother Hubbard a full loose gown for women.

Purty Boy Floyd infamous Depression-era bank robber; known for his kindness to poor people.

nestin' to place or settle; in or as in a nest.

speaking in tongues ecstatic or apparently ecstatic utterance of usually unintelligible speechlike sounds, as in a religious assembly, viewed by some as a manifestation of deep religious experience.

Chapter 9

Summary
The tenant people pick through their belongings, deciding what few precious items can be taken on the journey west. That which does not fit must be left behind or sold for a few miserable dollars. Buyers haggle over the tangible evidence of the tenants' existence: farming tools, dishes, furniture. They don't realize that they are acquiring not only "things" but also the tenants' past: their toils, their passions, and their bitterness. The most personal effects cannot be sold and must be burned. With their possessions stripped from them, the farmers are suddenly anxious to go. It's time to leave behind the old life, but not necessarily to begin a new one.

Analysis
The loss of dignity that results when the tenants are removed from their land is suggested in the thread of pathos visible in this particular chapter and woven throughout both the narrative and intercalary sections of the novel. Their dignity is trampled as they are forced to strip themselves of personal items, which by way of their connection with the land, define them. Shame, desperation, and fear characterize the families as they try to sell their belongings. "Two dollars isn't enough. Can't haul it all back." A similar attitude is taken by Pa in the next chapter as he worries about Ma's anger and disappointment when she learns they were only able to get 18 dollars for all their farm and household items. Taken away from the land that is their home, they are, figuratively speaking, dead.

In Chapter 8, Jim Casy and the Joads begin to grapple with the idea that only by banding together will the downtrodden be able to overcome the hardships that threaten their existence. The generalized characters of this intercalary chapter echo this development. The small man, in strong contrast to the group unity practiced by Ma and advocated by Jim Casy, is repeatedly exploited, hurt, and confused by a commerce system he doesn't understand. Although they realize they are being taken advantage of, they are powerless to help themselves. Cheated by buyers with unfair bargaining tactics, their anger begins to simmer. They are, as of yet, unaware of their collective power. Its promise, however, is emerging, and a warning is delivered, strongly reminiscent of the opening lines of "The Battle Hymn of the Republic" that "some day — the armies of bitterness will all be going the same way. And they'll all walk together, and they'll be a dead terror from it."

Glossary

gelding a castrated male horse.

premium an additional amount paid or charged.

Pilgrim's Progress a religious allegory by John Bunyan (1678).

St. Louis Fair the World's Fair of 1900 held in St. Louis, Missouri. The World's Fair is an exposition at which arts, crafts, industrial, and agricultural products of various countries of the world are on display.

Chapter 10

Summary

Ma shares with Tom her worries that the stories about California sound too good to be true. Granpa, however, can't wait to get to California where he will pick fruit and let the juice run down his body. Casy asks Ma and Tom if he can go west with them. Ma says she'd welcome him, but the menfolk have to decide.

The truck returns from Sallisaw later that afternoon. Ruthie and Winfield stand in the back of the truck with the pregnant Rose of Sharon and her husband, Connie. Pa and Uncle John are in the front seat, and Al, full of responsibility, is driving. They tumble out of the truck, tired and discouraged, having only gotten 18 dollars for all their household items, including the wagon.

That evening, the family meets by the truck for a family council where they decide that they will take along the preacher. Following the meeting, they all pitch in to slaughter the pigs, salt-pack the pork into barrels, and pack the rest of their possessions in the truck. With everyone working, the truck is loaded by daylight.

With Muley Graves to see them off, the Joads pile into the truck. At the final moment, Granpa refuses to leave. Ma puts some sleeping syrup in his coffee, and he is soon fast asleep. The men load him into the back of the truck, and the Joads start off. Ma tries to look back as they leave, but her view is blocked. The others in the back of the truck watch the house and barn until both are cut off from their sight, as the truck crawls westward.

Analysis

Chapter 10 marks the last time in the novel that the family unit will function as a traditional whole. Once the Joads leave Oklahoma, the family as a smaller unit will deteriorate and be replaced by a larger vision of community.

The Joads have a patriarchal family structure in which positions of leadership and control are determined by masculinity and age. Uncle John must sit in the front of the truck although he is uncomfortable and would rather give up his seat to the pregnant Rose of Sharon. However, "that would be impossible, because she was young and a woman." At the family meeting, Granpa is given the first chance to speak, which is his right as titular head of the family, even if his mind is no longer sharp. Once they leave the farm, a shifting in the family structure will weaken the power of these traditional gender roles. The tearing of the family from its agrarian roots is primarily responsible for this change in the structure of the family. Without the inherent responsibilities dictated by their farm-bound roles (the agricultural productivity of the men and the child-care and domestic duties of the women, for example), the Joads will lose their familial stability. Casy begins this process when he offers to help salt the pork, telling Ma, "It's all work. They's too much of it to split it up to men's or women's work."

The truck-side family conference illustrates the workings of family government, which will later be expanded into community government. Recalling the image of huddled men from Chapter 1, the Joad men take their well-scripted places in the family circle. For the first time, Al has graduated to a place among the squatting men. The women and children hover around the outside of the circle, although Ma is consulted on all decisions. Casy, not yet accepted into the family, maintains his distance from the gathering. The reader should note that the truck has become the center of the family and will symbolize its structure: Moments of mechanical failure will parallel the moments of loss and upheaval in the family.

The acceptance of Casy into the family marks the first time the lines defining the family are blurred. As a preacher, he has always been regarded as separate from the community he longs to be part of. His joining with the Joads is the first step for Casy in his desire to "be near to folks," and is indicative of the creation of a community that will take the place of the familial unit.

Granpa is the character most associated with the references to the "grapes" of the novel's title. Grapes in the novel are a symbol of both plenty and bitterness. At this point in the narrative, grapes represent the hope of plenty, the dream of a greater life. Even as Granpa is rejoicing in these possibilities, however, the seeds of bitterness are being sown. Stripped of their homes and personal effects, people are also stripped of their dignity. The frustration, loss, and fear felt by these people will turn to anger when they begin to collect together.

Glossary

handbill a small printed notice or advertisement to be passed out by hand.

single-action Colt a type of revolver invented by American Samuel Colt (1814-1862) — the hammer must be cocked by hand before each shot.

Salvation Army an international organization for religious and philanthropic purposes among the very poor.

muslin any of various strong, often sheer cotton cloths of plain weave; especially, a heavy variety used for sheets, pillowcases, and so on.

tappet a sliding rod in an engine or machine moved by intermittent contact with a cam and used to move another part, as a valve.

stereopticon a kind of slide projector designed to allow one view to fade out while the next is fading in.

singletree a wooden bar swung at the center from a hitch on a plow, wagon, and so on, and hooked at either end to the traces of a horse's harness.

signet ring a finger ring containing a seal, often in the form of an initial or monogram.

tarpaulin a waterproof sheet spread over something to protect it from getting wet.

Chapter 11

Summary
As the dispossessed stream out of the Plains land, the houses of the tenant farmers are left vacant. The only life left in the area is the shiny metal sheds that house the tractors. However, unlike the horse that continues to live after a day's work, the tractor is dead once its motor is turned off. This machine has made the job of the farmer too easy, so one can no longer wonder at the miracle of growth that rises from the land. Eventually, the houses die as well. Windows are broken, shingles loosened and tossed by the wind, until the only ones who disturb the dust on the floor are the wild animals from the fields.

Analysis
In this chapter, Steinbeck continues to draw a sharp contrast between the vitality of those who live close to the land and the mechanical lifelessness of those who use the soil for capital concerns. This theme is indicative of Jeffersonian agrarianism, which focus on the life-giving bond between human beings and the land with which they work. This theme is characterized by the sense of decay and death that hangs over the land abandoned by the farmers. Like the "muzzled" and "goggled" driver in Chapter 5, the man who runs the tractor goes home at night, distanced from the life growing in the fields he sows. Without the human element invested in the continuation of the life cycle, there can be no life. When the tractor is turned off, it dies. Similarly, when the farming families leave the region, they take life with them, which is symbolized by the wasting away of the vacant houses. Left to die, the houses are gradually taken over by nature, soon to revert to dust.

Glossary

corrugated iron sheet iron or steel with parallel grooves and ridges to give it added strength in construction.

Chapter 12

Summary
Route 66 is the main road of exodus for those fleeing from the harsh economic and environmental conditions of the Dust Bowl, stretching from the Mississippi to Bakersfield, California. Chapter 12 is a generalized vision of the harrowing journey west made by the displaced families. Thousands of people travel the highway, in constant fear over the state of their vehicles and their dwindling finances. Many are discouraged or run out of money. Their abandoned cars litter the highway. Yet, still more gather faith and strength from their fellow migrants and cling tenaciously to a narrow hope for a brighter future.

Analysis
This chapter provides a preview of the Joads' journey to California. Many elements that will be specified in the next narrative chapter are highlighted here. The constant plea for water foreshadows the water that will be forgotten by the family, and the blown tire (and subsequent search for a replacement) is indicative of the mechanical difficulties that the family will face. Even the warnings about going to California will eventually be addressed in the narrative. The positive ending of the chapter likewise anticipates more specific treatment. Just as a broken-down family is rescued and whisked to California by a generic benefactor, so the Joads lend a hand to the Wilsons. After fixing their car, the two families will also travel together in order to ease difficulties of the journey.

Steinbeck's prose style is influenced strongly by the King James Bible, and one of the strongest examples of this influence is in the narrative structure of his plot. *The Grapes of Wrath* can be divided into three specific sections: the drought and preparation to leave the farm, the journey to California, and the arrival in California. The juxtaposition of two chapters of general observation marks the respective end and beginning of these first two sections. Each of these sections can be paralleled with the experiences of the Israelites in the Old Testament. They correspond respectively with the oppression of the Israelites by the Egyptians, their exodus out of Egypt, and their eventual entrance into the land of Canaan. Steinbeck's description in this chapter of the Okies as "a people in flight" alludes specifically to this biblical story, while his listing of the towns on Route 66 recalls scriptural listings of genealogical lineages.

Chapter 13

Summary

As the car turns westward onto the concrete highway, Al is alert for signs of possible breakdowns. He asks Ma if she is frightened of what lies ahead in California, and she replies that her thinking about the future would be too much. She has to take care of what's in front of her.

At sundown, the family pulls over to camp, and they find themselves by Ivy and Sarah (Sairy) Wilson, a couple from Kansas, stranded with a broken-down car. Sairy is ill, but she and her husband welcome the Joads. Granpa becomes ill and, sheltered in a tent offered by the Wilsons, has a stroke and dies. Although full of grief, the Joads must decide what to do with Granpa's body. The law requires deaths to be reported, but that would cost the family forty dollars. They decide to bury Granpa in the night, although they are unhappy knowing that Granpa would hate anything so stealthy. Still, they need the money to get to California.

Granpa is buried in a quilt borrowed from Sairy, who also offers a blank page from the Wilson's family Bible so that Tom can write a note explaining the circumstances of his death, in case of the body's discovery.

During supper, Ivy Wilson explains how car trouble and Sairy's illness have hampered their progress and depleted their finances. Al and Tom offer to fix their car and propose that the two families travel together, sharing the cars. At first the Wilsons are reluctant, but Ma convinces them it is better to work together.

Analysis

A moment of foreshadowing is found in Ma's conversation with Al when she responds to his concern about bringing Casy along with them to California, "You'll be glad a that preacher 'fore we're through." Their decision to include the preacher into their family will prove fortuitous immediately, when he is called upon to help with Granpa's funeral, and more importantly later in the story, when he gives himself up to a sheriff so that Tom is not jailed.

Granpa's death and the "adoption" of the Wilsons in this chapter reveals a change in the family structure that supports the theme of social unity: The concept of the individual family is being replaced by a larger concept of a world family. Granpa's death is the first loss the family endures, and it is instrumental in drawing the family together as a unit. As a group, the Joads — and now also the Wilsons — must decide what to do with their corporate family body, and in deciding, create their own laws based on what Casy refers to as the "have-to's." This group government dynamic, already witnessed in the family conference in Chapter 10, will be seen in greater scope in the government camp in California. The "adopting" of the Wilsons into the family furthers the concept that communal unity is necessary for survival. Several symbolic gestures unite the two families: Granpa dies in the Wilson's tent, Sairy Wilson's quilt is used to wrap his body, and a page torn from the Wilson's family Bible is buried with him. In deciding to travel together, the two families instinctively fulfill Casy's speculation that it is only by working together that they can survive the trek to California. As Ma puts it, "Each'll help each, an' we'll all git to California."

The occasion of Granpa's death reveals Steinbeck's dissatisfaction with organized religion and illustrates Casy's pragmatism. Pragmatism, which focuses on what "is" as opposed to what "ought to be," is one of the aspects of Steinbeck's social theory. Casy's unconventional blessing over Granpa's body contrasts the impracticality of religion and prayer with the practical nature of the new human-based spirituality: The people who are still living in this world are the ones in most need of faith and support.

Granma is the prime representative of this useless spirituality. She is glad the preacher is along, not because she thinks he will be of help to the family, but because he can say grace in the morning. When Granpa is suffering through his stroke, she is almost beside herself as she demands of Casy, "Pray, goddam it." Granpa dies as Casy haltingly says the Lord's Prayer, knowing it isn't going to make a difference. Prayer is inadequate in dealing with daily life. His attitude is summed up in a comment he later makes to Tom in the Hooverville camp, "I use ta think that'd cut 'er . Use ta rip off a prayer an' all the troubles'd stick to that prayer like flies on flypapr, an' the prayer'd go a-sailin' off, a-taken' them troubles along. But it don' work no more."

Tom's conversion is not yet imminent, yet he finds in his willingness to humor Casy's speeches the possibility of gaining wisdom. Casy can be seen as symbolic of Christ, and Tom is often considered Casy's disciple. Tom continues to remain proud and independent, but the ex-preacher is pricking his consciousness. He is frustrated with a service station owner because he refuses to listen to Casy, but his innate compassion takes over when he understands the service man will soon be on the road just like them. Tom's intuitive response to the idea that all are in this together helps him realize that the service man's circumstances are similar to their own.

Glossary

touring car an early type of open automobile, often with a folding top, seating five or more passengers.

pauper any person who is extremely poor.

Chapter 14

Summary
The United States is nervous as change begins. The great owners try to blame these changes on obvious things, like the growing labor movement or new taxes. They are unaware that these changes are the *results* of circumstances, not the *causes*. The causes are much more basic: Hunger, not just in one stomach, but in millions, and the desire of men to work and be productive. This need to produce beyond the work itself, to suffer and die for a belief is the foundation of human nature.

Analysis
Chapter 14 documents the beginning of a social shift; a gradual emerging of social consciousness from "I" to "We" begins to emerge. In the previous chapters, Steinbeck chronicles the circumstances responsible for the growing anger and bitterness of the dispossessed. Frightened, tired, and hungry, these wandering people begin to join together, victims of the same circumstances, the gradual recognition of the gathering migrants that there is strength in uniting together. Acting upon Casy's belief that love between fellow humans is the key to holiness, these squatting migrants begin to share what little they have with each other. With these actions comes the realization that by banding together, they will survive. Ma's statement to the Wilsons in the preceding chapter sums up this attitude, "Each'll help an' we'll all git to California." It is the first cell of a growth in community made stronger by actions of individuals.

The chapter also intensifies the conflict introduced in Chapter 5 between the powerful bank or company and the small farmer. The drive of the powerful owners to produce a profit, first illustrated by the removal of the tenant farmers, is threatened by the common people who want only a place to settle and live. In this chapter, we see these dominant owners blinded by their own greed. They sense that a change is imminent, but Steinbeck suggests that their insulation from the land prevents them from understanding the undeniable power that will arise from the development of a like-minded community of disenfranchised people.

Glossary

Paine, Thomas (1737-1809), American Revolutionary patriot, writer, and political theoretician, born in England.

Marx, Karl (Heinrich) (1818-1883), German social philosopher and economist, in London after 1850, founder of modern socialism.

Lenin, Vladimir Ilyich (1870-1924), Russian leader of the Communist revolution of 1917, premier of the U.S.S.R. (1917-1924).

Jefferson, Thomas (1743-1826), American statesman, third president of the United States (1801-1809), drew up the Declaration of Independence.

squatters persons who settle on public or unoccupied land.

Chapter 15

Summary
Hamburger stands line Route 66. In the kitchen, the male partner — in this chapter, Alyheru4 — is generally silent and does not acknowledge the diner's patrons. Mae, representative of the woman behind the counter, usually middle-aged and talkative, is the link between the paying public and the business.

Out on the highway, cars and trucks from all parts of the country stream by, all of them traveling west. Inside expensive cars are worried, portly businessmen with languid wives. They are going to California simply to be able to impress the folks back home. When they stop at the diner, they irritate the woman behind the counter by wasting napkins, complaining, and not buying anything.

Two truck drivers stop at the diner. While talking to Mae, they describe an accident in which a truck, laden with mattresses and cookware and kids, was struck by a reckless driver. Meanwhile, another car brimming with household goods pulls off the highway, and a man and his two young boys enter the diner to ask for 10 cents worth of bread. She refuses at first, offering to sell him a sandwich. The man is resilient in his humility, explaining that they have budgeted carefully in order to make it to California and can only afford a dime. Eventually, Al yells at Mae to simply give them the bread. As the man is leaving, he sees the boys eyeing peppermint candy and asks if it is penny candy. Mae replies that it is two for a penny, although it is really nickel candy. The man buys each boy a stick and leaves. The truckers, realizing what Mae has done, pay their bill and each leaves a 50-cent piece although pie and coffee is only 15 cents.

Analysis
Chapter 15 is the most fully realized of the intercalary chapters, becoming somewhat of a microcosm of the book as a whole. With alternating intercalary paragraphs, the chapter shifts between the generalized and the specific, moving from broad descriptions of roadside diners and a wide variety of highway travelers to the specific story of Mae and Al. Recalling the symbolic position of the diner in Chapter 2 and Chapter 13, Mae and Al are both curiously connected and insulated from the world that is rapidly passing on the highway outside their door. Their business is their base, the solidity of which is protection from migratory hazard. At the same time, their survival is entirely dependent on the choice of travelers to stop at their restaurant. Their reputation among the traveling community is critical to their life.

The complicated system of support illustrated by this chapter is an example of the community unity expounded by Casy. Mae, like Tom, will go through something of a mini-education, as she realizes that individual survival is impossible. Acting toward one's fellow human with compassion and respect is necessary to survive. The incident with the man and the loaf of bread illustrates this concept. Mae is, at first, unwilling to sell a portion of the loaf to the migrant man. Shamed into a sale by Al, she seems to see the impoverished, yet proud, man and his children for the first time. Gruffly, but not unkindly, she sells nickel candy to the man two for a penny. Her act of compassion is rewarded by the truck drivers who witness it and leave her a large tip. By sharing with others one can accumulate strength, and in this case, rewards.

The chapter also offers a different perspective of the people moving west. The wealthy travelers, symbolic of the great owners, are unproductive and spoilt. They whiz by on the highway, encapsulated from each other and from the road. The woman, fat and unproductive, with her sagging breasts lying fallow in her lap, contrasts directly with Rosasharn who is filled with unborn life. Even though Rose of Sharon's child will be stillborn, her breasts will provide life-giving milk for another member of the larger world family. The isolation of these individuals signifies the barrenness of life lived separately from one another. We are also given a glimpse of how the migrant families were viewed by others. In the initial response of the diner's hostess to the migrant man, we see through the eyes of those established people who fear the strength and desperation of those on the move.

Glossary

lodge a local chapter of a fraternal organization.

service clubs clubs, such as Rotary and Kiwanis, organized to provide certain services for their members and to promote the community welfare.

syphilis an infectious venereal disease usually transmitted by sexual intercourse or acquired congenitally.

Chapter 16

Summary
For two days, the Wilsons and the Joads are in flight across the Panhandle, leaving Oklahoma and crossing Texas. Eventually, they became accustomed to their traveling way of life. As they drive through New Mexico, Rosasharn tells her mother about her and Connie's plans once they reach California. They want to live in town, with Connie taking correspondence courses and getting a job in a factory or store. Ma voices her concern that she doesn't want the family to split up, but realizes that it is just a dream.

A rattle in the engine causes Al to pull the car over and discover a broken connecting rod bearing. They anticipate a time-consuming repair, and Tom suggests the family go ahead to California to find work. He and Casy will stay behind, fix the car, and then catch-up with the others in California. The others reluctantly agree with the plan, but Ma refuses to leave. She picks up a jack handle and says she will beat anyone who makes her split up the family. Faced with her immovability, the others give in.

Al takes the family up the road to a camp, while Tom and Casy remove the connecting rod. Tom and Al find a junkyard and retrieve a matching con-rod from a wrecked car. They are able to get the car fixed that night and meet up with the family at the camp. The roadside camp charges a 50-cent fee to spend the night. Tom refuses to pay, preferring to sleep outside on the road. He parks the car outside the gate and walks in to talk to his family. Pa is sharing the family hope for work in California with a group of men when a stranger emerges from the shadows to tell his own sad story. Unable to find work in California, the stranger's wife and two children had starved to death. Pa is worried and asks the preacher if that is the truth. Casy answers that it's the truth for him, but he doesn't know what the truth for the Joads will be. Tom and Casy speak briefly with Ma and plan to meet up later in the morning. Tom, Uncle John, and Casy go out to sleep on the road.

Analysis
In this chapter, we see how the deterioration of the Joad family parallels the downward spiral of their economic fortunes. Granpa, unable to tear himself from the land, died the moment they left the farm. Without Granpa, Granma's health also fails rapidly, and Rosasharn shares that once they get to California, she and Connie want to branch out on their own. Ma sees her family crumbling and begins to fight desperately to keep them together. Her desperation to keep the family together is so great that she responds to any immediate threat with drastic measures. When the broken-down car prompts Tom to suggest that the family split up for a short time, Ma reacts with violence, grabbing the jack handle and demanding the family remain intact. She realizes that outside forces are tearing them apart; without their home, nothing is left

to bind them together. With this recognition, Ma again restates the theme of survival through group unity, "All we got is the family unbroken. Like a bunch of cows, when the lobos are ranging, stick all together."

With Ma's revolt comes a shift in familial power. Although she had deferred to the men in the group, Ma had always been a reckoning force in the family structure. Recall that at the truck-side family conference she had roamed the perimeter of the men's circle, but decisions were not made without her input. Yet it must be noted that Ma was not an early feminist. Quite clear about her traditional role as comforter, nurturer, and protector of the family, she also realizes that something of Pa's strength was taken when he lost the ability to provide for his family. For the sake of family unity, she must temporarily take control.

Tom's anger toward the camp proprietor for capitalizing on the misfortune of the migrant families echoes Steinbeck's attitude concerning the crimes of profit-hunters. Humans must not work for independent benefit, but for the good of all, a concept that recalls the tractor driver in Chapter 5, who chose to put other families off their farms in order to earn three dollars a day to feed his own family. The owner recognizes this attitude in Tom, calling him a "troublemaker," but Tom, like Steinbeck, is not really advocating communism in the strict sense. Much more important is the theme of humanism, of helping out others who are trapped by hard times, the personal expression of the theory of love expounded by Jim Casy. At the same time, Steinbeck is not suggesting that everyone should receive a free ride because they encounter unfortunate circumstances. Earlier in the chapter, Tom had taken to task the one-eyed man in the wrecking yard because he was feeling sorry for himself. Hard work is important, and Steinbeck goes to great pains to reiterate the desire of men to work, to sweat, and as Casy says, "Fling their muscles around and get tired."

This chapter also provides a somewhat critical crossroads in Tom's spiritual conversion, which critic Warren French has called his "education of the heart." While fixing the car, Casy begins to share with Tom observations that recall the prophetic images of the previous intercalary chapter: "[Them people] ain't thinkin' where they're goin' — but they're layin' 'em down the same direction, just the same. They's gonna come a thing that's gonna change the whole country." These reflections frustrate Tom as they force him to consider larger social issues and his own part in them. He's not ready to do that, preferring to think only of his own immediate future. It's clear, however, that Casy's teachings are beginning to tug at his innate compassion. Upon reaching the roadside camp, he stands up against the profiteering proprietor, subconsciously shifting from, "If I pay I ain't a vagrant," to "We ain't asked ya for nothing." Like Muley and Ma before him, Tom is beginning to learn he has no other choice but to become involved.

Glossary

panhandle a strip of land projecting like the handle of a pan. Here refers to the western extension of Oklahoma.

con-rod bearing a reciprocating rod connecting two or more moving parts of a machine, as the crankshaft and a piston of an automobile.

babbitt a soft white metal of tin, lead, copper, and antimony in various proportions, used to reduce friction as in bearings.

shim a thin, usually wedge-shaped piece of wood, metal, or stone used for filling space, leveling, and so on, as in masonry.

jack [old slang] money.

proprietor one who owns and operates a business establishment.

Bolshevicky here refers a member of the Bolshevik party, a majority faction (*Bolsheviki*) of the Russian Social Democratic Workers' Party, which formed the Communist Party after seizing power in the 1917 Revolution.

Chapter 17

Summary

As the cars of the migrant families travel west, they begin to create their own communities with rules, laws, punishments, and social expectations. A community begins with one family camping alongside the road. Eventually, one family turns into 20 families. As the families camp together, it becomes clear that each person has certain rights, such as the right to food and to privacy. Likewise, other things are unacceptable, such as being noisy when the camp is quiet or eating food while another goes hungry. These things are punishable by fighting or ostracism. In the morning, the families pack up just like a traveling circus and continue out on the road to California.

Analysis

Chapter 17 provides an abstract illustration of the re-formulating concept of community, a generalized vision of people governing themselves by adhering to a philosophy of living not unlike Casy's theory of love and the Oversoul. We are all part of one being; therefore, if we all follow laws (or rights) that arise out of common sense, experience, and respect for others, it is possible to govern ourselves. This idea of self-governing migratory camps will be solidified in the government camp at Weedpatch. These pockets of self-government are in sharp contrast to the laws enforced by those in power — laws designed to keep weaker persons at a disadvantage. It is this injustice that Tom is fighting against when he later rages against cops and other formal figures of authority.

The theme of survival by pragmatism is illuminated by the inhabitants of these transitory, self-governing camps. Those people who are able to be flexible, to adapt to new circumstances, are the ones who will survive, and adaptability is gained through group action. People isolated into "I" thinking are static, while those who join together to create a "we" community are always shifting, always changing. We should remember that Steinbeck's novel is not just a social tract for its time — the solutions he offers are neither radical, nor one-sided, but universal. Although he strikes a sympathetic cord in his heartfelt description of injustice, he also asserts that it is not enough for the economic powers to "play fair." In order for society as a whole to survive, fair industrial practices must be met by changes in the moving forces of people.

Glossary

Dutch-oven a metal container for roasting meats, with an open side placed so that it is toward the fire.

migrant a farm laborer who moves from place to place to harvest seasonal crops.

Chapter 18

Summary

The family moves westward through Arizona and arrives weary in California at dawn. At mid-morning, they camp along the banks of the Colorado River, where Tom and the men bathe and decide whether or not to cross the desert that night. Granma is ill, but Pa, worried about the money, wants to get work as soon as possible. While bathing, they speak with a man and his son returning from California. They explain the hardships that await the Joads: fertile ground lying unplanted, job scarcity, and corrupt owners who cheat the workers. Hardest to bear is the hostility of the natives who have derogatorily labeled the newcomers "Okies." Although the Joads are frightened, they have no choice but to go on. They finish their bathing and decide to nap on the shore before continuing their journey that evening. Noah follows Tom into the brush and tells him that he won't be going on to California with the family. He's going to follow the river and fish. He asks Tom to tell Ma.

In the tent, Ma and Rosasharn sit with Granma, whose health continues to deteriorate. A large woman offers to hold a Jehovite holy meeting for Granma, but Ma refuses, insisting that Granma is just worn out from the heat and travel. Ma and Rose of Sharon rest for the night's trip, but are awoken by a local authority who warns them to be gone by morning, because the town doesn't want any "Okies" settling down there. Ma, angry at being spoken to so disrespectfully, threatens him with a skillet. After he leaves, Ma sits and tries to compose herself.

To avoid trouble, the family decides to move on immediately. Knowing that the trip across the desert will kill Sairy, the Wilsons decide to stay. The Joads go on by themselves, leaving the Wilsons some food and a few dollars. During the night drive across the desert, Ma continues to lie with Granma and comfort her. Midway through the trip, agricultural inspectors want to inspect the truck for produce, but Ma begs hysterically to be able to continue. She explains that Granma is very ill and must see a doctor. The inspector allows them to go on.

They drive through Barstow and up over the mountains. As the truck descends into Tehachapi, the family is struck by the beauty of the valley below. Al stops the truck, and the family piles out to look at California. Ma tells everyone that Granma has died, has been dead, in fact, since before the agricultural inspectors stopped them. She couldn't help Granma because she knew the family had to get across the desert. The family is awestruck by the strength of her love.

Analysis

As her family continues to crumble, Ma's strength, drawn intuitively from love, continues to grow, making her a physical symbol of the humanism strand of Steinbeck's social theory. The family is disintegrating as the Joads are forced to leave the Wilsons behind, Noah refuses to leave the water at the Colorado River, and Granma dies. Ma fights against this destruction, defending her clan against mounting intrusions and circumstances.

When the religious woman at the camp offers to pray over the ill Granma, Ma sends her on her way, preferring to keep the privacy of her family. She is stung by the venomous intrusion of the sheriff who warns her that they don't want any "Okies" settling down and she responds physically, threatening him with a skillet. Unable to defend Granma against death, she chooses to put the needs of the living ahead of those who have passed. Keeping quiet about Granma's death, she allows the family to get across the desert. Casy's response when he learns about her heroism stands as a definition of Ma's character, "There's a woman so great with love — she scares me."

With each strike against the family, Ma's strength is doubled, but her desperate desire to maintain the family will be thwarted the longer they stay in California. Although she is considered a symbol of human love, it is a love of family above all others that she practices. As the family's economic plight worsens, Ma can do nothing to keep them together. She will be forced to replace her immediate family with a world family, one that includes the entire community.

Glossary

shuck to remove a shell, pod, or husk.

fallow land plowed but not seeded for one or more growing seasons, to kill weeds, make the soil richer, and so on.

Okie a migratory agricultural worker, forced to migrate from Oklahoma or other areas of the Great Plains because of drought and farm foreclosure in the 1930s.

Jehovites members of a proselytizing Christian sect founded by Charles T. Russell (1852-1916).

exhortation a plea or sermon urging or warning people to do what is required.

feral untamed; wild.

Sam Browne belt a military officer's belt with a diagonal strap across the right shoulder, designed to carry the weight of a pistol or sword.

epaulets shoulder ornaments for certain uniforms, especially military uniforms.

Tehachapi mountain just east of Bakersfield.

heliograph a permanent image formed on a glass plate by an early photographic process.

Chapter 19

Summary

When the Americans first came to settle in California, they were hungry for land. Driven by a desire for property, they dominated the complacent Mexican natives, successfully stripping them of their claim to this fertile farmland. Soon, these Californians were no longer squatters, but owners. Farming became an industry, not a passion, and success was measured in dollars only. Farms became larger and owners fewer.

As the dispossessed come to California, they bring with them a wild, desperate hunger for land. History had told them that when all land is held by a few, it is taken away. And when great masses are going hungry, while a few are well fed, there will be a revolt. In an effort to diffuse the strength of the migrant workers, the owners make laws, and law officials enforce them. Any man farming on a small strip of land is charged with trespassing, and squatter's camps — "Hoovervilles" — are closed and burned for being a threat to public health. Meanwhile, children in the Hoovervilles are dying from hunger while their parents pray for food. When the parents stop praying and start acting, the end for the owners will be near.

Analysis

Together with Chapters 21 and 23, this chapter presents historical background on the development of land ownership in California, tracing the American settlement of the land taken from the Mexicans. Fundamentally, the chapter explores the conflict between farming solely as a means of profit making and farming as a way of life. Steinbeck criticizes the industrialization of farming in which a love of the land is replaced by a capitalist mentality. With the advent of this industrialization came a shift toward commercial farming. With the focus only on the moneymaking aspects of growth, the corporate farmers increasingly exploit immigrant and migratory workers who are willing to work for a low wage. Like the machines that pushed the sharecroppers off their land, these great landowners had "become through their holdings both more and less than men." A key image of agrarian sympathy is found in the patch of jimson weed. Here Steinbeck effectively illustrates the crimes committed by the frightened owners with a picture of a hungry migrant stealthily clearing a jimson weed patch so that he might grow a few vegetables to feed his family, only to have it gleefully destroyed by a local sheriff.

A distinct contrast is also made here between existing immigrant workers (the Chinese, Mexican, and Filipinos) and the recently arrived "Okies" who feel strongly that they are Americans. Perceiving themselves as coming from a similar background as the rest of the inhabitants of the Golden State, the "Okies" insist on similar rights. This knowledge that they deserve the same decencies as any other American citizens gives strength and credence to their demands and makes them appear more dangerous to the California natives.

Glossary

serfs persons in feudal servitude, bound to a master's land and transferred with it to a new owner.

straw bosses supervisors who have little or no authority to support their orders.

dispossessed deprived of the possession of something, especially land, a house, and so on.

barbarians people regarded as primitive, savage, and so on.

Hooverville any of the encampments of displaced persons especially prevalent during the 1930's; "Hoover" is a reference to the President of the United States at the time, Herbert Hoover.

jimson weed a poisonous annual weed.

Chapter 20

Summary

The family takes Granma's body to the coroner in Bakersfield but can only spare five dollars for her burial. The family stops at the first tent camp they see on the outskirts of town, a settlement of tents, each with a vehicle parked next to it. As the family sets up camp, they meet Floyd Knowles, a young man in the neighboring tent who explains the harassment tactics of the police. If they think that anyone is heading up a group of workers, they will put that man in jail, and anyone who speaks out against the injustice of the law is killed. No one cares because the victim will simply be listed as a "vagrant found dead."

Tom takes his leave of Floyd and returns to his family's camp where Ma, surrounded by a group of ragged children, prepares a stew. Casy tells Tom that he will move on so as not to burden the Joads any longer. He promises to repay their hospitality. Tom asks him to stay at least one more day, as he has an uneasy feeling trouble is brewing. In the tent, Connie is sullen, telling Rosasharn he should have stayed in Oklahoma and studied about tractors. He will leave, never to return. Ma learns that none of the children standing around have had any breakfast. Ma dishes out the stew to her family, but leaves what's left in the pot for the children.

After dinner, Tom and Al return to help Floyd. As they talk, groups of men drive into the camp, discouraged and tired from not finding work. A few minutes later, a shiny car drives up. The driver emerges and offers the men jobs picking fruit in Tulare. Floyd responds that when he writes down what the wage will be, signs it, and shows the men his contractor's license, they will sign up for the work. Angry, the contractor and his companion, a deputy, accuse Floyd of breaking into a used car lot and try to arrest him. Floyd strikes the cop and flees the camp. The deputy shoots at him, wounding a nearby woman, and is tripped by Tom. He continues to shoot and is kicked in the neck by Casy, rendering him unconscious. Tom cannot afford to get in trouble with the law because of his parole, so Casy offers to take the blame. Tom hides near the river when the cops return. Casy turns himself in.

As the sun lowers, Al goes in search of Tom, and Ma begins supper. Uncle John tells Ma and Pa that he has sinned by withholding five dollars to get drunk with, but they tell him that this is not a sin since the money is his. Rumor has it that the Hooverville will be burned that night, a common ploy of the local authorities to halt any organizing. When Tom returns from his hiding place, the family collects the drunken Uncle John and decides to go to the government camp at Weedpatch. As the truck leaves camp, they are stopped by cops who tells them to go north to Tulare. Tom wants to resist, but is restrained by Ma. The strain of being servile is beginning to show on Tom who momentarily sobs. Reasoning that the cops can't tell a person where to go, Tom turns around, cuts through town, and continues south toward Weedpatch. They leave behind the crackling sounds of flames as the Hooverville is destroyed.

Analysis

Agrarian philosophy, a strong component of Steinbeck's social thought, is symbolized by the desire of people to be close to the land. In this chapter, Casy, like many of the novel's characters, facilitates his thinking by placing his feet in the dirt. This image is rampant throughout the narrative, from the small children of Chapter 1, who "draw figures in the dust with bare toes," to Tom Joad, whose first gesture on the road to home is to take off his shoes and wiggle his toes in the dirt.

Jim Casy is quite clearly understood to be a Christ-figure in the novel. Most obviously, his initials, J.C., are the same as Jesus Christ, but the symbolism is present in other forms. Like Christ, he goes into the wilderness to experience a spiritual rebirth, and in this chapter, he sacrifices himself for Tom. Through this sacrifice, this symbolic giving of his body, he will be opened to a full understanding of the group unity philosophy he has been working toward.

This chapter marks the moment Casy stops talking and begins acting. His giving up of himself for Tom is immediately foreshadowed when he tells Tom, "I ain't doin' nobody no good." Within hours, he will have the opportunity to begin doing good, carrying out his theoretical ideals by kicking the deputy and sacrificing himself for Tom. This move signals an active embracing of the pragmatic thought that is so integral to Steinbeck's social philosophy.

Casy's sacrifice marks a counter movement in Tom's conversion. Unlike Casy, who is moving from thought to action, Tom is working in the opposite direction: Unable to act (to get work or improve his family's situation), Tom is forced to observe and reflect. Up until this point, he hasn't paid much attention to Casy's ideas because they hadn't been relevant in day-to-day existence. Now, however, he begins to grasp Casy's ideals as well as his own social responsibility. This conversion from what scholar Peter Lisca calls a private, inner morality to an outward expression of morality will be finalized when Tom is forced to hide out in the cave, and he is shackled into complete inaction.

The movement toward a community unity builds in this chapter as the traditional family unit is replaced by a larger, world family unit. As the Joad's economic situation declines, the family unit suffers more loss. Casy, Granma, and Connie are now gone. The global family unit, however, is beginning to be forged by an outward extension of love, represented by the sacrifice of Jim Casy, the exchange of help between Al and Floyd Knowles, and Ma's feeding of the hungry children.

Glossary

coroner a public officer whose chief duty is to determine the causes of any deaths not obviously due to natural causes.

embalming the process of treating a dead body with various chemicals, usually after removing the viscera, to keep it from decaying rapidly.

"on-relief" aid in the form of goods or money given, as by a government agency, to persons unable to support themselves.

belligerently in a hostile or quarrelsome manner.

vagrant one who wanders from place to place without a regular job, supporting oneself by begging.

stir-bugs [slang] prison inmates.

coupe a closed, two-door automobile.

flagged sent (a message) by signaling.

self-abasement a humbling or abasement of oneself.

kerosene lamps lamps that burn kerosene, a thin oil distilled from petroleum or shale oil.

servile humbly yielding or submissive.

tunics short coats worn by soldiers, policemen, and so on.

Chapter 21

Summary
Endless streams of people move out on the highways, like ants searching for food. These are agrarian folks, pushed off their land by great machines. As they flow toward the west's fertile fields, hunger and desperation change them. The people who live in the towns the travelers pour into are frightened. These townspeople do not own the land, but they work and have debts, and they are frightened by the hunger-filled desperation of these nomads, wanderers who would work for any food to fill their families' empty stomachs. The great owners of the fields buy the canneries as well and underbid the small farmer, forcing him to ruin until he, too, joins the rivers of the hungry. And the great owners think that they can take advantage of these desperate folks, but they don't realize that it is "a thin line between hunger and anger."

Analysis
Steinbeck uses this intercalary chapter to continue his attack on commercial farming methods and their utter disregard for human decency. His sympathy for an agrarian lifestyle is characterized by his angry description of the ploy of larger companies to buy canneries and then underbid, and eventually destroy, the small farmer.

The perceived threat of the Okies to the California natives is examined once again as the result of basic decencies denied to a large number of people by a powerful few. The desperation among the hordes of displaced workers has grown to such a level that even the store clerks know they must fight to protect their own small holdings.

Both Chapters 21 and 25 make use of a biblically influenced prose style that resonates with angry admonishes and wrath. By maintaining an extended allusion to Julia Ward Howe's "The Battle Hymn of the Republic," which Steinbeck had planned at one time to have printed somewhere in the novel, these two chapters create a mood of apocalyptic reckoning. The context of the book's title in the song refers to the Book of Revelation (Rev. 14:19), "The angel swung his sickle on the earth, gathered its grapes and threw them into the great winepress of the God's wrath." Steinbeck's wife actually chose the title for the novel, although the author was pleased with the choice because he valued its American emphasis and believed it would offset both fascist and communist criticisms or identities, according to biographer, Jackson Benson. The first four lines of the song are, "Mine eyes have seen the glory of the coming of the Lord, / He is trampling out the vintage where the grapes of wrath are stored; / He hath loosed the fateful lightening of his terrible swift sword, / His truth is marching on." Steinbeck describes the armies of bitterness marching in Chapter 9 and ends this chapter with a warning that the anger of the migrant workers is beginning to "ferment." He continues these allusions in Chapter 25.

Glossary

repel to drive or force back; hold or ward off.

pustules small elevations of the skin containing pus.

pellagra a chronic disease caused by a deficiency of nicotinic acid in the diet and characterized by gastrointestinal disturbances, skin eruptions, and mental disorders.

ferment to excite; agitate.

Chapter 22

Summary
After leaving the burned out squatter's camp, the Joads go to a government camp where community-elected officials make camp decisions, create laws, and hand out punishments. The next morning, the Joads' new neighbors, Timothy and Wilkie Wallace, invite Tom to work with them. The owner for whom they are working tells them he must lower their wage, or the bank will not renew his crop loan. He also warns the men that the Farmers Association will cause a fight at the government camp dance so that there will be a reason for deputies to close the camp.

The manager of the camp welcomes them, and at first Ma is suspicious. He is kind and respectful, though, and Ma relaxes with the realization that she is among her kind of people again. The men leave to look for work, while Ma and Rosasharn clean up in preparation for the Ladies' Committee visit. While Ma is washing up, an older woman from the camp, a religious fanatic, tells Rose of Sharon that sinful things are happening in camp, including dances and plays. She warns the girl that two other young women have lost their babies because of their sinful behavior. Rosasharn panics, but Ma reassures her. When the Ladies' Committee arrives at the Joad tent, they explain to Ma the rules of the camp and the workings of Sanitary Unit Number Four. The Joad men return unsuccessful in their search for work. Ma tells Pa that now that the family has stopped moving, she has time to remember the sad things, such as Granpa's death and Noah's leaving. She and Pa reminisce about Oklahoma, but stop themselves when they remember that it is no longer their home.

Analysis
The respite experienced by the Joad family while at Weedpatch marks the high point of the narrative's parabola of action. Here, Steinbeck's vision comes together — humans governing themselves without an endless cycle of fear and domination. Not only does the government camp exemplify the ideal in humane group management, it stands in contrast to the camp the Joads have just left, the demoralizing and squalid "Hooverville." Ma is welcomed into the community with respect, and human dignity is momentarily restored as people are made to "feel like people" again.

Another instance of humanism is the pre-dawn breakfast to which Tom is invited. Not only do the Wallaces offer food, they also invite Tom to share their work. This invitation will shorten the length of their own employment, but it echoes the communal attitude of the camp. This attitude is also supported by the small owner, Mr. Hines, who warns the men of a plan by the Farmers Association to spark a riot at the camp's dance. He represents the small owners described in the preceding intercalary chapter. Indeed, forced to lower his wages by pressure from the Farmers Association, Mr. Hines will eventually be put out of business by the large farming corporations.

Glossary

shirtwaist a woman's blouse or bodice tailored more or less like a shirt.

clout power or influence.

red agitators political radicals or revolutionaries, especially applied to Communists, who stir up people in support of a cause.

bandanna a large, colored handkerchief, usually with a figure or pattern.

pone cornbread in the form of small, oval loaves.

disconsolately so unhappy that nothing will comfort; inconsolable; dejected.

gingham a yarn-dyed cotton cloth, usually woven in stripes, checks, or plaids.

skitters slang term for diarrhea.

croquet an outdoor game in which the players use mallets to drive a wooden ball through a series of hoops placed in the ground.

mallet a long-handled hammer with a cylindrical wooden head, used in playing croquet.

Chapter 23

Summary
The migrant people search for pleasures as they search for food and work, a necessity for survival during the hard times. They tell stories to one another, some made-up, some from the movie pictures. Those with a little money get drunk to deaden the pain of their situation. Others play music: Harmonica, guitar and fiddle; bands are formed and dances held. Young people dance to release their energy and older members of the community clap and tap their toes. At the end of the evening, the young dancers pair off and go out into the darkness.

Analysis
This relatively light-hearted intercalary chapter prefigures the camp dance to take place in the next narrative chapter by describing the various diversions enjoyed by the migratory people despite their daily hardships. The various aspects of folk culture and character are woven together in the music, dance, and group forms of entertainment of these people who have been thrown together by circumstances.

Glossary

Geronimo (c. 1829-1909), Apache Indian chief.

newsreel a short motion picture of recent news events, shown as part of the program in motion picture theaters.

Cherokee a member of a North American Indian people formerly inhabiting a large area of the south Allegheny Mountains, now in Oklahoma and North Carolina.

Chapter 24

Summary

On a Saturday, the entire camp prepares for the evening's dance. The Central Committee meets to discuss ways to prevent the Farmers Association from stirring up trouble. The men at the gate of the camp will look out for anyone suspicious, and extra members are added to the entertainment committee. Ezra Huston, the chairman, warns that troublemakers must not be harmed physically because any altercation would only give the deputies a reason to shut down the camp. Tom is recruited by the committee to help ward off any trouble.

That evening, Ma is able to convince Rose of Sharon to go to the dance by promising that she won't allow anyone to bother her. At the gate, Tom and Jule, a camper of Cherokee blood, spy three suspicious young men entering. They follow them to the dance floor where they try to start a fight. As planned, the entertainment committee forms a wall around them and escorts them from the floor. The men are recognized as migrants, and Mr. Huston sadly wonders why they have turned against their fellow workers. They are taken out and forced to leave, unharmed. The committee returns to the dance.

Pa, Uncle John, and other men meet to talk about work possibilities. One man shares the story of mountain men in Akron, Ohio, who were being exploited by the rubber factories. They attempted to organize a union, but the townspeople tried to run them out. The mountain men held a "turkey shoot": On a Sunday, five thousand men walked through town with guns. The man feels the Okies ought to have a "turkey shoot."

Analysis

The prevention of a fight at the dance is an example of group action as it is most effective. The group proves they can work together to achieve a common goal, but it is also clear that the ability to organize well is more likely to happen when people are allowed to be clean and treated with respect. A measure of dignity must be provided in order for social advancements to be made. The success of this group action elaborates precisely why the large landowners are frightened by the migrants. Given the opportunity to work together, these "Okies" demonstrate they are not stupid or lazy like the powers that be would prefer to believe. They are a proud, productive, and potentially powerful group of people, and for this reason, the land owners would like to destroy any camps that promote any kind of organization.

The peaceful solution to the interruption at the dance becomes ironic by the end of the chapter. Peaceful solutions may work well when people can bathe and feel safe, but outside the gates of the government camps, the anger of the dispossessed is beginning to ferment. The anecdote shared at the end of the chapter concerning the revolt of workers against the rubber companies in Akron, Ohio, is a prelude to the violent action of the strike that will take place in the next chapter. The man in the black hat concludes his story of the workers' "turkey shoot" with an observation about their own labor situation: "They're gettin' purty mean out here. Burned that camp an' beat up folk. I been thinkin'. All our folk got guns. I been thinkin' maybe we ought to git up a turkey shootin' club an' have meetin's ever' Sunday." Circumstances are coming to a head, and the time has come for thought to be put into action. The response to this call to action will be seen in the strikebreaking efforts of Jim Casy as he attempts to put into practice the beliefs we have seen develop throughout the story.

Glossary

sidled moved sideways, especially in a shy or stealthy manner.

rakishly dashingly; jauntily.

two bits [informal] 25 cents.

Chapter 25

Summary
The California land is ripe with growing produce. The toil and ingenuity of many men create this bountiful harvest: Growers strive to learn better techniques for yielding succulent fruit, and chemists experiment with pesticides to protect crops from insects and disease. But the large landowners drive the price of labor down, and the small farmer, who pours his sweat and passion into the land, cannot afford to harvest it. He must turn his holding over to the great companies. The food that cannot be gathered must be destroyed. If hungry people are allowed free food from the fields, store prices will plummet. Crops are burned as hungry people watch, their anger mounting.

Analysis
One of the strongest and most poetic of the intercalary chapters, Chapter 25 opens with the beautiful image of spring coming to the farms of California, and ends with a warning message of biblical retribution, resonating with a tone of moral and physical decay.

In keeping with his agrarian philosophies, Steinbeck continues to rail against the misuses of machinery and industrial power, although he has praise for those scientists who have labored to increase the bounty of the harvest. We should remember that Steinbeck was not anti-technology: His preoccupation with machinery for both positive and negative ends can be seen in many places throughout the novel. What was unconscionable to Steinbeck, however, was the use of the land for profit only, disregarding the life force that grows out of it. For those seeking only capital gains from the land, he has dire prophecies. As a result of the ruin forced upon the ripening harvest, children are dying. The interruption of one life cycle must interrupt another life cycle.

The chapter culminates with an apocalyptic contrast between land used for life-giving nutrients and land manipulated for profit. As in Chapter 23, Steinbeck concludes here with a reference to the "Battle Hymn of the Republic" and speculation that a revolution of the people cannot be far off.

Glossary

quarantine any isolation or restriction on travel or passage imposed to keep contagious diseases, insect pests, and so on from spreading.

graft the act of taking advantage of one's position to gain items such as money and property dishonestly, as in politics.

cultivators implements or machines for loosening the earth and destroying weeds around growing plants.

putrescence the state or condition of something that is decomposing or rotting.

denunciation a public accusation or strong condemnation of someone or something.

Chapter 26

Summary

After spending a month in the Weedpatch camp, the Joad men have been unable to find any sort of work. The family is running out of food, and Rose of Sharon's baby is due soon. Ma decides that they need to leave the camp to search for work. Her assumption of leadership angers Pa, but Ma continues to goad him. Her sassing is calculated to rile him up, figuring that if a man has something to get angry at, he'll be okay.

The Joads leave the government camp early the next morning. While fixing a flat tire on the truck, a well-dressed man offers them work as peach pickers. When they arrive at the Hooper Ranch, policemen escort them through wire gates. Angry, shouting people surround the entrance. Inside the gates, the Joads are registered and begin picking fruit for five cents a box. The entire family works and by sundown they have earned a dollar. Ma spends the dollar at the Hooper Ranch store but can only get some poor quality hamburger and a little coffee. The sales clerk is sarcastic, but Ma recognizes his shame. She asks for some credit in order to get a little sugar, but the clerk refuses. Surprisingly, however, he pays for the sugar and tells her to bring the credit slip so that he can get his dime back. She tells him she is learning that if "you're in trouble or hurt or need — go to the poor people. They're the only ones that'll help."

After supper, Tom attempts to find out what had angered the crowd of people around the gate. Slipping out of the ranch, he comes across Jim Casy in a roadside camp. Casy has been in jail and shares with Tom what he has learned about the effectiveness of group action by observing his fellow inmates working together. The ex-preacher then explains that he and the others in the camp are striking against Hooper Ranch. They were promised wages of five cents a box and then given two-and-a-half cents a box. The Joads are being paid five cents because they are strikebreakers. Once the strike has been squelched, the wage will be dropped.

As Casy is explaining this, they are met by a group of men with weapons and flashlights. They strike Casy in the head with a pick handle and kill him. Tom immediately grabs the handle and beats Casy's killer. He is struck in the face but is able to run away. Tom hides in the orchard until he can make his way back to the ranch.

The next morning, Tom tells the family what he has done. Knowing he would be recognized because of his broken nose, he stays in the house with Rosasharn while the rest of the Joads work. With Casy's death, the strike is broken, and the wage has been dropped to two-and-a-half cents a box. The family returns from their day of work with only $1.42. Winfield collapses because of dysentery he got from eating peaches. Pa tells Tom that he is being hunted, and there is talk of lynching. Tom wants to leave, but Ma won't let him. Once dark falls, they hide Tom in the truck and leave the ranch.

Al turns the truck north, keeping to the back roads to avoid any cops. They pass a row of boxcars and a sign that says, "Cotton Pickers Needed." The family agrees to get work picking cotton and hopefully, stay in one of the boxcars. Tom will hide down by the stream, near enough that Ma can bring him food each night. He'll remain there until his face heals.

Analysis

Jim Casy's sacrificial act of going to jail for Tom was symbolic of his position as a Christ-figure, a symbolism that is strengthened in this chapter. While in jail, Casy sees the effectiveness of group action and attempts to relate this to Tom in the form of a parable about sour beans. His jail experience brought a full realization of his beliefs and spurred him to carry out these ideals. When Tom finds him, he is doing just that, leading a strike for a living wage. Like Christ, he will be killed to save his people, his dying words ("You don't know what you're a-doin'") paraphrase Jesus' dying words. Prior to his death, he attempts to get Tom to return to the camp and spread word of the strike to the workers. Tom refuses, not yet ready for this discipleship, but after Casy's death and a long period of reflection, he will be able to continue the work that Casy has begun.

Pa's decline and Ma's assumption of the leadership role within the family illustrate the negative inversion of Steinbeck's theme of human dignity as a product of human identity with the land. With Pa unable to provide for his family, he falls into moments of passivity and confusion. At the opening of the chapter, Ma must force the others to confront their situation. The government camp offers safety, but not work or food. Intuitively understanding that Pa needs to be angered in order to find his strength, she uses her impudence to spur him to action. After Tom has killed Casy's murderer, Ma again directs the family to hide Tom and leave the Hooper Ranch. She has no intention of taking over the traditionally masculine role of head of the household. Her only concern is maintaining the wholeness of her family. She longs for the day when they can be safe and together so that she might relinquish the leadership position and return to the traditionally accepted family structure.

Glossary

strike a concerted refusal by employees to go on working in an attempt to force an employer to grant certain demands, as for higher wages, better working conditions, and so on.

union something united or unified; a whole made up of parts; esp. an organization or confederation uniting various individuals, political units, and so on.

to act flip [colloq.] to act flippantly or impertinently.

J.P. Morgan (1867-1943) U.S. financier; known as "Jack," to distinguish from his better-known father, J.P. "Pierpont" Morgan.

haycocks small, conical heaps of hay drying in a field.

vigilantes members of vigilance committees, groups that keep order or punish crime without legal authority.

strikebreaking the act of one who attempts to break up a strike, often by intimidating striking workers.

win'fall peaches here refers to windfall peaches; something blown down by the wind, as fruit from a tree.

Depression the period of economic depression which began in 1929 and lasted through most of the 1930s.

lynchin' to murder (an accused person) by mob action and without lawful trial, as by hanging.

culvert a pipe-like construction of stone, concrete, or metal, that passes under a road, railroad track, footpath, or through an embankment.

boxcars fully enclosed railroad freight cars.

Chapter 27

Summary
Cotton pickers are wanted. Even if a worker doesn't have a bag, he can buy one and pay for it with his pickings. Many of the migrants are comfortable picking cotton, remembering home. Sometimes the scales are crooked, and sometimes they're not. For the most part, people are paid a decent wage, and at the end of the day, they can provide meat for their family.

Analysis
Steinbeck returns to the now-familiar newsreel literary technique in this chapter, with a staccato-styled collage of voices speaking of the migrants' experience in picking California cotton. Both the tone and the action prefigure the Joads' experiences picking cotton in the next chapter. The tone is uplifted because men are working again, earning enough to put some meat on the table. They spread their good fortune around, helping each other, sharing information about weighted scales. Their happiness is cautious, however, because they know that winter is coming, and work will end. The Joads, too, will enjoy a momentary respite before their misfortunes pile up again.

Glossary

bolls the roundish seed pods of a plant, especially of cotton or flax.

Chapter 28

Summary

The Joads are one of the first families to get work picking cotton, so they are able to live in one of the boxcars. They share this dwelling with another family, the Wainwrights. The Joads are able to earn enough money to have meat each night and are able to buy some new clothing and some Cracker Jacks for the children.

While Ma is cooking supper that evening, Winfield rushes in to tell her that Ruthie has gotten into a fight and childishly boasted to the other children that her big brother was hiding because he had killed two men. Ma is instantly concerned. Leaving the others to eat, she goes to the hidden culvert to warn Tom.

She meets Tom who takes her back to the lightless cave he has been hiding in. Explaining what Ruthie has done, she tells him that he'll need to go far away. Tom agrees. Ma hasn't seen Tom since he has been in hiding, and there is no light in the cave, so she touches his face to remember him. He tells her that while he has been alone, he has thought a lot about Jim Casy and what he taught.

Tom is beginning to grasp the preacher's idea that people must stand together. He realizes that each person doesn't have their own soul, but rather is a piece of a great big soul that includes everyone, and "his little piece of a soul wasn't so good 'less it was with the rest, an' was whole." He doesn't completely understand this philosophy, "it's jus' stuff [he's] been thinking about." Ma begs him to find the family later on, but Tom tells her that if Casy's theory is true, she'll find him in every human action around her: "Wherever there's a fight so hungry people can eat, [he'll] be there." He wants to continue the work that Casy had begun. When Ma expresses her worry that they will kill him like the preacher, Tom replies, "He didn't duck fast enough."

Returning to the boxcar, the Wainwrights approach Ma and Pa with concerns about Al and their sixteen-year-old daughter, Aggie, spending time together. Ma and Pa agree to speak with Al. Once the Wainwrights leave, Pa confides to Ma that he feels like life is over and done. Ma reassures him that they will keep on going. Aggie and Al return from a walk to announce they want to get married and live on their own. Ma begs them to stay until spring, and the families celebrate.

The next morning, both families leave for the cotton fields before dawn, knowing that this will be the end of the work for the season. When they arrive, people are already in line. With so many people, the fields are picked by 11:00 a.m. As they return home, the rains begin, and Rosasharn takes a chill.

Analysis

While Tom is in the cave, he experiences a re-birth: The completion of his spiritual conversion from an independent, self-centered individual to someone who must take action to share his morality with all persons. Confined to the cave, Tom is forced into silence and inactivity and is finally able to reflect on the words of Casy. He understands, for the first time, Casy's theory of human love and survival, the concept that all persons share one soul and cannot exist alone. With this understanding comes a new awareness that Tom has a social responsibility to help all those in need. In keeping with his symbolic position of discipleship, it is important to note that only after Casy's death does Tom reach a point in his conversion that he might emerge from hiding to carry Casy's message to the masses.

The symbolism of the cave in which Tom hides is suggestive of the theme of re-birth and recalls his refusal to sleep in the cave with Muley Graves. The cave is symbolic of the womb, implying that Tom is preparing to be spiritually re-born, leaving his current family to embrace all of humankind. Ma must go down a narrow passage to reach him, and darkness is pervasive. Reminiscent of her reaction to Tom's homecoming in the beginning of the novel, Ma feels Tom's face in the dark. Her actions are a form of farewell and signify the break with his immediate family, a break that is necessary for him to begin ministering to the needs of the larger world family.

Glossary

Cracker Jack trademark for a confection of sweet, glazed popcorn and peanuts.

cynically in a manner that indicates a belief that people are motivated in all their actions only by selfishness.

cord any force acting as a tie or bond.

cat-walk a narrow, elevated walk or platform, as one along the edge of a bridge or over the engine room of a ship.

salts refers here to smelling salts; an aromatic mixture, used as an inhalant in relieving faintness, headaches, and so on.

drawers underpants with either short or long legs.

Chapter 29

Summary
The gray clouds bring torrents of rain to the land. Eventually, the earth can hold no more water and the streams rise, flowing into fields, which in turn become lakes. The migrant workers helplessly watch the rising water. As the lands flood, their cars are incapacitated, and worst of all, there is no work. The workers are unable to get government relief because they have not lived in the state for a year. Weakened by hunger, many resort to begging and stealing. The pity of the townspeople for the starving workers soon turns to fear. The only person in town who is busy is the coroner.

Soon the rain stops. The men come out and squat down, surveying the land and thinking, while the women watch to see whether this is the time they will finally break. But, where men sit in a group, talking, fear leaves their faces and is replaced by anger. And the women know their men will not break if they are angry.

Analysis
This final intercalary chapter serves as a partner to the novel's opening chapter by repeating several key motifs. The scrolling description of the weather and its effect on land is virtually the same except, instead of drought, Steinbeck is chronicling the spread of the floods. The circle of squatting men figures prominently as well, a tribute to the indomitability of the life force symbolized by the land turtle in Chapter 3 and illustrated in Rosasharn's gift of life-saving milk in the closing chapter. As in the first chapter, the woman worry that their men will break under the strain of accumulated hardships, but now there is a difference: Where two men squat together, fear turns to anger. As long as they can work together, they will be able to survive.

Glossary

freshets a sudden overflowing of a stream because of melting snow or heavy rain.

crags steep, rugged rocks that rise above others or project from a rock mass.

Chapter 30

Summary

Pa and Uncle John, realizing that the rising water will eventually flood the cars, ask the other boxcar dwellers to work together to build an embankment to stem the water. They know it will take the strength of all the men working together. If some refuse, all will have to leave. With the support of the Wainwrights, the men leave to talk to the other campers.

Although she is not due yet, Rosasharn begins to have labor pains. When Pa returns, Ma tells him Rose of Sharon's time is come. He is spurred to action, telling the men that the bank must be put up because his girl is having her baby. The men work feverishly in the downpour. As their labor continues through the night, they can hear screams coming from the Joad's car. Soon after the screams abate, a large cottonwood tree, uprooted by the flooding, topples onto the bank, ripping a hole that allows the water to pour through. Al and the others race to their cars, but are unable to start them before the automobiles are surrounded by water.

Utterly dejected, the men return to the car to find that Rosasharn's baby is born dead, shriveled and blue from lack of food. It is only a matter of time before the car floods, so Al suggests building a platform to keep their belongings dry. They spend the night huddled on the platform.

In the morning, Ma insists they leave to find higher ground. Al stays with Aggie and the Wainwrights. Carrying Rosasharn, Winfield, and Ruthie, Ma, Pa, and Uncle John set out along the flooded road. Drenched by a cloudburst, they decide to take shelter in an old barn. Once inside, they realize that they are not alone — a boy is kneeling next to the body of his father.

The boy tells Ma that his father is starving. The weakened man cannot keep down anything solid, but must have some nourishing liquid like soup or milk. Ma looks to Rose of Sharon, and as their eyes meet, there is silent agreement. Ma takes the rest of the family out of the barn, while Rose of Sharon sits next to the father. Loosening the blanket that covers her body, she offers her full breast of milk to the dying man. As he drinks, a mysterious smile appears on her lips.

Analysis

Rosasharn's gesture in the closing lines of the novel can be considered a completion of the life cycle, an act that reaffirms the themes of re-birth and survival. In giving a part of herself to a stranger, she experiences a spiritual movement that extends beyond herself and unifies her with the vast human family. This act also recalls the Christian ritual of Holy Communion in which the body and blood of Christ is shared among believers. More strongly, it illustrates the culmination of what Peter Lisca has called the "education of the heart": The development from a inward focus on nourishment and self-sacrifice for the protection of the family to an awareness that we are all part of a larger community in which life-giving resources are shared.

A loss of immediate family seems to be a prerequisite to understanding one's place as part of a global community in which all persons are a part of one great soul. Casy, the first to consciously understand this concept, was never part of a family unit. He begins by wondering "what they is for a fella so lonely?" and finds the answer in joining together with all men and all women. Likewise, Tom reaches this understanding when he is permanently isolated from his family. He tells Ma that even if he cannot regain contact with his own family, he will survive because he is now part of the large family of humanity. Just as the truck, a symbol of the vitality of the family throughout the narrative, is flooded and rendered useless, by the end of the novel, there is virtually nothing left of the Joad family. Yet it is at this moment that they will be forced to put into action Ma's accepting statement that their responsibility extends beyond immediate relations, "Use'ta be the fambly was fust. It ain't so now. It's anybody. Worse off we get, the more we got to do." Rose of Sharon's gesture, expressed to a man who reminds us of Granpa, unifies the Joad family as they initiate their membership in the vast human family.

Glossary

levee an embankment built alongside a river to prevent high water from flooding bordering land.

eddied moved with a circular motion against the main current.

cottonwood a rapidly growing lowland tree.

fetid having a bad smell, as of decay.

intermittent stopping and starting at intervals.

gaunt thin and bony.

CHARACTER ANALYSIS

Tom Joad

While many have long believed that Jim Casy embodied Steinbeck's main philosophical beliefs, Tom Joad, completely flawed and human, is the novel's main character. Tom is the character who shows the most development, experiencing what Peter Lisca calls an "education of the heart." This education, gained through experience, intuition, and the teachings of Jim Casy, best exemplifies the moral journey from self to community, from "I" to "we." Tom moves from caring only for himself to a familial loyalty to seeing the entire world as his family.

Tom is kind and often merciful, yet quick to anger and fiercely independent. As a man of action, he embodies one of the novel's main philosophical strands, pragmatism, standing in contrast to the idealistic and talkative Jim Casy. While Casy is predominantly an observer and commentator on the human condition, Tom's acts of humanity are subconscious, his insights and compassion intuitive. Tom is concerned with the practical aspects of his life as they relate to the here and now, not the moral or ideological circumstances surrounding his actions. In this sense, Tom and Casy follow inverted paths in the development of their characters. After Casy has the opportunity to witness his beliefs acted out by the jail inmates, he moves from a position of observation and contemplation to one of action. Tom's social role moves in the opposite direction, from one of action to one of reflection. Not until Tom stops moving and reacting does he have the opportunity to absorb Casy's ideas. When he does so, however, Tom's development comes full-circle as he pledges to return to continue the actions begun by Casy.

Ma Joad

The emotional and physical backbone of the family, Ma's primary obligation is to take care of her family, to provide them with nourishment, comfort, healing, and support. Her family will only know fear and pain through her, so she works hard to deny these emotions in herself. Likewise, they look to her for laughter, so she builds joy out of small moments. Above all, however, her calm, unflappable strength binds everyone together. Ma finds this strength in love. She is the embodiment of Casy's idea of love, possessing the same intuitive sense of morality that Tom has. Although her primary focus is to take care of her own family, she is the first to nurture others. As Casy observes, "She don't forget nobody."

During the Joad's trek to California, Ma, in her desperation to maintain family unity, finds her role expanding. As crisis threatens to tear the family apart, she shifts to a position of active leadership. With each assault against the unity of her clan, she gradually takes over Pa's role as head of the family. When Tom suggests splitting up the family, she threatens him with the jack. While camped at the Colorado River, she wields a skillet when confronting an officer who orders the family to leave, although her greatest concern is that he will anger Tom. She forces the family to action in the Weedpatch camp and keeps Pa strong by giving him something to fight against. In the end, it is Ma who demands they leave the boxcars for higher ground.

This is not to say that Ma desires to be the leader. Her function within the family remains rooted in traditional feminine traits of nurturing and protection, and her primary desire is to "keep the fambly whole." She wishes nothing more than to reach a place where they can be a family with clear, logical boundaries. Her attempts to school Rosasharn in the way to be a strong woman, keeper of the family, reinforces Ma's attitude toward her function within the family framework.

Jim Casy

A traveling preacher, Jim Casy was "lousy with the spirit" but troubled by the sinful sensuality that seemed to result from being "all full up of Jesus." He leaves preaching and wanders in the wild country, trying to come to terms with his own ideas about God, holiness, and sin. When we first meet him, he is still struggling with these concepts, but is beginning to narrow them down to an earthy interpretation of Emerson's theory of the Oversoul: All souls are just a small portion of a larger soul, this larger soul being the "Holy Sperit the human sperit." Being part of this holy spirit means accepting all parts of people, thus "there ain't no sin and there ain't no virtue. There's just stuff people do. It's all part of the same thing." Realizing that these ideas will not be accepted in traditional worship, Casy has declared himself no longer a preacher, although he continues to be a speaker and teacher. Specifically, he shares his theories with Tom, who is an impatient, but not unwilling listener. At various points, Casy's teachings reflect the various philosophies of transcendentalism, humanism, socialism, and pragmatism.

Jim Casy is the moral spokesman of the novel and is often considered a Christ-figure. The initials of his name, J.C., are the same as Jesus Christ, and like Christ, he wanders in the wilderness. In Christ-like fashion, Casy sacrifices himself when he turns himself in to save Tom after an altercation with a deputy. Prior to this point in the novel, Jim has been primarily a speaker, more worried about figuring things out than acting on his ideas. His sacrifice for Tom marks the first time that Casy acts. For his sacrifice, Casy in put in jail, where his experiences with the positive effects of group organization lead him to a more complete realization of his beliefs. He leaves jail and begins to put his theories into practice. He dies a martyr's death, paraphrasing Christ's last words ("Forgive them, Father, for they know not what they do") when he cries, "You don' know what you're a-doin." And, like Christ, his teachings are delivered to the rest of the world as the result of this death. Tom, who must be considered Casy's disciple, vows to spread his message as he works toward greater social justice.

Rose of Sharon Joad

Petulant and imbued with an inflated sense of self-importance, Rose of Sharon is the least likeable of the characters. A young newly-wed, she and her husband spend the journey to California giggling softly and dreaming of the possibilities of their new life. Her constant concern is that everything that happens to the family is related somehow to her unborn child, a concern that quickly becomes annoying. Despite her mother's interventions, Rose of Sharon (reduced to Rosasharn by her family) draws increasingly into her own self-pity as the family's hardships mount. The bearing of her stillborn child, however, brings about a change in her character. Her breasts are full of life-giving milk and with no child to nourish, Rose of Sharon chooses to reach beyond her own considerations for the first time. She offers her milk to a stranger, a man dying of starvation. With this act, Rose of Sharon comes to represent the full circle of human unity: Despite her own position of need, she is able to give life.

Pa Joad

Not as roundly developed as Ma, Pa represents the theme of the loss of human dignity. Losing the farm seems to "take somepin' out of Old Tom," and now that he can no longer provide for his family, he often seems lost or bewildered. At the beginning of the story, Pa is still the head of the family and, as such, is given due respect. However, as the family meets with increasingly difficult situations, he begins to relinquish his role as leader to Ma or Tom, depending on the situation. Pa is no longer able to provide in the traditional sense, and this renders him alternately angry or passive, but rarely productive. In the stories Tom tells, and in Tom's own character, we catch a glimpse of what Pa was probably like before being tractored off his land: strong, suspicious of strangers, fiercely independent, and capable of a murderous temperament when pushed around.

Other Characters

Al Joad
The teen-aged brother of Tom is a social young man, his primary concerns being girls and cars. He admires Tom, particularly because he has been in prison, and until the family reaches California, strives for his older brother's approval. Because he had "driven truck" for a year, Al is given the responsibility of maintaining the family's automobile, a responsibility he takes seriously. Although a pleasant, well-meaning young man, he lacks Tom's sense of morality and accountability. For example, while Tom is investigating the commotion outside the gates of the peach ranch, Al's main objective is searching out available young girls. Although Al never seems to experience a spiritual conversion on the scale of his brother Tom, he does grow in ways that are significant to Steinbeck's message of social change. His engagement to Aggie Wainwright at the close of the novel indicates a joining of the Wainwright and Joad families, an act symbolized by his taking down of the curtain separating the two halves of the boxcar. This joining is only temporary, however, as Al will be left behind when the Joads abandon the boxcar. Aggie and Al, in their desire to create a non-agrarian life outside of their families, represent the ability to change that Steinbeck feels is necessary for the survival of the migrant worker.

Granpa Joad
Granpa is a colorful old character — earthy, lecherous, and full of life. He is somewhat of a child, shouting and behaving outrageously, bragging about what a "heller" he was, and swearing. He forgets to button up his trousers after using the bathroom. At the beginning of the story, Granpa is the one character who seems completely ready to embrace a new life (he speaks of crushing grapes and letting the juice run down his face). But ironically, when it is time to depart, he refuses to leave the land on which he has lived his entire life. Granpa has to be drugged to be taken off the property and is never again completely conscious after the family leaves. When the family makes camp at the end of the first day of travel, he has a stroke and dies.

Granma Joad
Equal to Granpa in crotchetiness and spirit, she loves to argue with him. She is comically spiritual — an example of the absurdity of organized religion. She shouts "PRAISE GAWD" every time Casy pauses during grace, even though it's not grace in the conventional sense. Her clinging to her spirituality is seen most poignantly at Granpa's death when she frantically demands of Casy, "Pray, goddam you." After Granpa's death, she retreats into a somnambulistic state, becoming increasingly incoherent. She dies during the Joads' nightlong trek across the California desert and is buried a pauper when the family reaches Bakersfield.

Uncle John Joad
Pa's older brother, John has, for many years, carried the responsibility for the death of his young wife during her first pregnancy. Midway through her pregnancy term, she had complained of stomach pains. John refused to get a doctor, because he was sure she had simply "Et too much." By the next afternoon, she was out of her head with pain and soon died from a burst appendix. Wracked with remorse for this "sin," John alternates between drunkenness and widespread acts of haphazard charity. He lives with the burden of this individual sin, which seems to become overwhelming during times of family crisis.

Ruthie Joad
At 12 years old, Ruthie is poised between childhood and adulthood. She is often childish and domineering, particularly of her younger brother. Her bossy attitude makes it difficult for her to make friends in the various camps the family stops in. In fact, during a fight with another child, she spills the information that her brother Tom is hiding nearby because he has killed a man.

Winfield Joad
Ten-year-old Winfield is the youngest member of the Joad clan. He and Ruthie seem the least affected by the leaving of the family home. Winfield is, for the most part, a typical child: boisterous and playful.

Noah Joad
The eldest Joad son is quiet and strange, but not retarded, as he would seem at first glance. He can read, write, and figure as well as the others, but he is oddly detached, even from his family. His role in the family is an understated one. When the family camps at the Colorado River, Noah decides that he can't leave the water and becomes the first member to consciously abandon the family.

Ivy and Sarah (Sairy) Wilson
The Joads meet this migrant couple on the first night of their journey. Looking for a place to camp, they roll up next to the Kansas couple's disabled automobile. When Granpa dies of a stroke, the Wilsons offer their tent space and quilt. They even tear a page from their own bible to be buried with Granpa. In return, Al fixes their car, and the two families decide to travel to California together. They remain together until the California desert when Sairy tells her husband that she is too ill to continue. The Joads leave the couple, knowing that she will not survive. The Joads' relationship with the Wilsons is a microcosm of the larger picture of migration, a look at the strength derived from unity in action. Their communal way of life is amplified in scope at the government camp at Weedpatch.

The Wainwrights

The Wainwrights are another migrant family looking for work in California. They share a boxcar with the Joads on the ranch where they pick cotton. Like the Wilsons, the Wainwrights represent the necessity of working together to form one community in order to survive. During the rains, Mrs. Wainwright helps Ma deliver Rose of Sharon's stillborn baby, and Mr. Wainwright helps Pa to build the embankment to stem the flood. Forced to drop familial boundaries, the Joads learn to accept help as well as to give it. When Al becomes engaged to the Wainwright's daughter, Agnes, he tears down the cloth separating the two halves of the boxcar, symbolically creating one family.

CRITICAL ESSAYS

Use of Literary Devices in the Intercalary Chapters of *The Grapes of Wrath*

The unconventional structure of *The Grapes of Wrath*, in which the narrative chapters are interspersed with intercalary chapters of general comment or information, has frustrated and annoyed readers right up to the present day. Many complain that the chapters are interruptions in the story proper, or that they split the novel into two distinct sections only loosely related. The discerning reader, however, will agree with Steinbeck's claim that the structure of the novel was indeed carefully worked out. Employing a variety of literary styles and techniques, Steinbeck is able to cross-reference details, interweave symbols, and provide outside commentary on narrative events in such a way that the two types of chapters blend together, unifying and enhancing the social and humanist themes of the novel. According to Steinbeck scholar, Peter Lisca, the author uses three specific literary devices to minimize disruption and bring together the two components of the novel: juxtaposition, dramatization, and a variety of prose styles.

One technique used to unify the separate parts of the novel is juxtaposition. Details are consistently and repeatedly inter-related between narrative and intercalary chapters. Most often an intercalary chapter will present a generalized situation that will either become more fully realized or brought to a conclusion by the events in the succeeding narrative chapter. For example, Chapter 7 provides the monologue of a used car salesman and is followed in Chapter 8 by an account of the Joads preparing to leave, having just purchased a used Hudson Super-Six. Similarly, Chapter 29, which describes the relentless rains that flood the California valley, is framed by the first drops of rain falling at the end of Chapter 28 and the floods that threaten the Joads' boxcar in Chapter 30. The repetition of key elements, often symbolic or thematic in nature, also works to integrate the two types of chapters. The land turtle, whose symbolic struggle across the highway is meticulously described in Chapter 3, is picked up by Tom Joad in Chapter 4 and released in Chapter 6, only to continue its journey in the direction soon to be followed by the Joad family. In the same way, the family rescued by the benevolent stranger at the end of Chapter 9 foreshadows the "rescuing" of the Wilsons by the Joads in the next chapter.

A second technique, perhaps most widely used in the intercalary chapters, is that of dramatization: The use of a collage of vignettes, monologues, and dialogues designed to show the social and historical processes behind the events that were occurring in the story of the Joads. In Chapter 9, for example, we hear the frustrations of the farmers forced to sell their belongings through an economic system they don't understand, strengthened with the repeated comment, "Can't haul 'em back." Similar to medieval mystery plays that brought biblical stories to life for the understanding of the common people, Steinbeck uses generalized characters and dialogue to illustrate the plight of the dispossessed tenants. Not wishing to merely tell about social or historical facts that composed the backdrop of his plot, Steinbeck allows his readers to find out for themselves the effect of the drought on the sharecroppers, or the gradual deterioration of the houses abandoned by farmers forced to migrate westward.

The dramatically differentiated prose styles used in the intercalary chapters allows Steinbeck to soften the chapters' somewhat moralizing tone and avoid the accusation that they could be grouped together as their own separate section of the novel. The newsreel style of a contemporary of Steinbeck's, author John Dos Passos, is seen in the used car salesman chapter, while the depiction of the boy and his Cherokee girl dancing in Chapter 23 is almost cinematic. The earthy, folk language employed by the Joads, Wainwrights, Wilsons, and other characters in the primary narrative is echoed in the comments of the generalized characters in the intercalary chapters. In keeping with the purpose of these chapters as general expansions of specific events, however, quotation marks indicating precise speakers are quite obviously absent. These conversational collages strengthen the function of these intercalary chapters to provide an overview of the social situation affecting the Joads.

The most striking and pervasive style used in these intercalary chapters is language and rhythms reminiscent of the syntactical structures of the King James Bible. With its force and authority, this biblical voice, present in both the opening description of the drought and the closing description of the floods, becomes the moral center of the novel. The spiritual beauty and strength of this language is most clearly seen in the apocalyptic warning delivered in Chapter 25, "There is a crime here which goes beyond denunciation. There is a sorrow here that weeping cannot symbolize. There is a failure here that topples all our success. The fertile earth, the straight tree rows, the sturdy trunks and the ripe fruit. And children dying of pellagra must die because a profit cannot be taken from an orange."

Separately, these intercalary chapters have moments of brilliance and beauty. However, it is the way in which they are intricately, and inextricably, woven into the fabric of the primary narrative that they most confirm the genius of Steinbeck's highly personal and global vision of humanity.

Philosophical Influences on Steinbeck's Social Theory

According to Frederick I. Carpenter in his essay, "The Philosophical Joads," Steinbeck's social thought seems to be shaped by three distinct strands of nineteenth century American philosophy: the Emersonian concept of the Oversoul, the idea of a humanism expressed by the love of all persons and the embracing of mass democracy found in the works of Walt Whitman and Carl Sandburg, and the pragmatism of Henry James.

The Transcendental concept of the Oversoul is expressed in the earthy folk language of Jim Casy as the belief that all human's souls are really just part of one big soul. Ralph Waldo Emerson, the most well known proponent of transcendentalism, defined the Oversoul as the universal mind or spirit that animates, motivates, and is the unifying principle of all living things. Casy makes numerous references to this one large soul that connects all in holiness, and they dovetail nicely with the basic idea of strength in group unity. Somewhat conversely, American transcendentalism also recognized individualism, a faith in common people and their self-reliance. This concept of the survival of the human life force is symbolized by the survival of the land turtle and Ma's comment, "We're the people — we go on." This combination of rugged individualism and an embracing of all men as part of the same Great Being is physically expressed in the education and re-birth of Tom Joad: His strongly individual nature gives him the strength to fight for the social welfare of all humanity.

The movement of the major characters in the novel from a religious-based to a humanity-based philosophy of life supports the concept of humanism found in Steinbeck's social theory. This thought reflects the political ideals of the nineteenth century American poet, Walt Whitman, who believed that democracy was based on the existence of a mutual connection between individuals, a situation in which the group entity was of as great an importance as the individual. Humanism can be traced back to Whitman's exaltation of the common man and can best be understood as a love of all persons. This is the spirit that Jim Casy is referring to when he claims that it's "all men and women that we love the Holy Sperit — the human sperit." This love will most often be physically expressed by the mother figures in the novel: Ma, Sairy Wilson, and eventually, Rose of Sharon. From her first appearance in the novel, Ma is the epitome of the concept of loving one's neighbor. She is the first to extend comfort or nourishment to strangers. This willingness to help people is seen in her welcoming of Casy into the family and her feeding of the hungry children in the Hooverville camp. She works selflessly for others and tries to instill the same attitude in Rose of Sharon. Sairy Wilson's compassionate help during Granpa's death, in spite of her own illness, is another example of human love extending outside the family. Rose of

Sharon is slow to embrace this selflessness and giving, focusing instead on her own comfort and well-being for the majority of the novel. In the end, however, she, too, becomes part of this embracing of all humankind when she offers her life-giving milk to the starving stranger.

The third strand of Steinbeck's philosophy is pragmatism, what the author himself has termed "non-teological" or "is" thinking. Pragmatism holds that life should be viewed as it is, not as how it ought to be. Accordingly, one needs to live in the moment, reacting to what is happening in front of them based on their life experience and personal judgment, not on religious or moral teachings. Tom's responses to most situations are highly pragmatic, focused on "doing" as opposed to seeing or thinking. He is frustrated by Casy's broad musings on the future, preferring to "lay [his] dogs down one at a time" and "climb fences when [he] got fences to climb." He imparts this attitude to Ma, cautioning her to "Jus' take ever' day." Ma, however, is a pragmatist in her own right, but her pragmatic focus is on keeping her family together. When Al asks whether she is thinking about life is California, she is quick to reply that the others depend on her thinking only of their safety and comfort. Completely understanding her role in the family, she takes each setback as it comes and modifies her actions according to whatever situation confronts her. This ability to be flexible is another aspect of pragmatism, an ability that Steinbeck feels is fundamental to the survival of the migrant workers. Pragmatism also includes a movement away from abstract religious beliefs, concentrating instead on the holiness of those who are living. Casy's acceptance of this belief is seen in his abandonment of formal religion and prayer. His comments at Granpa's grave, that those who are living need help, support his pragmatic attitude.

The theory of Jeffersonian agrarianism was later recognized by critic Chester E. Eisinger to be the fourth strand of Steinbeck's social philosophy. Agrarianism is a way of living that is intricately tied to one's love and respect of land. Through connection with the growth-cycle of the land, humankind gains identity. Steinbeck's symbolic treatment of this idea can be found repeatedly in *The Grapes of Wrath*. Steinbeck uses the life force in a horse and the mechanized power of the tractor to metaphorically contrast the productiveness that comes from a love of the land with the deadness that arises from an isolation from it. Men are whole when they are working with the land, and conversely, they are depleted, emotionally and physically, when they are taken from the land. Losing the farm "took somepin' outa Pa," and one displaced tenant states, "I am the land, the land is me." When that land is taken away, the men lose part of themselves, their dignity, and their self-esteem. Also closely tied to the land is family unity. With the separation from the land comes a disintegration of the family unit. Ma expresses this most succinctly when she observes, "They was the time when we was on the lan'. They was a boundary to us then. We was the fambly — kinda whole and clear. An' now we ain't clear no more."

STUDY HELP

Quiz

1. How does Granpa Joad die?
A) He dies in a fight during a workers' strike.
B) He dies of heat exhaustion.
C) He has a stroke.
D) He suffers a heart attack.

2. Siary Wilson's offering of shelter to the Joads and Ma's feeding of the hungry children in the Hooverville reflect a strand of philosophy that is closely tied to Walt Whitman's concept of love for all individuals. Which of the following is the name of that philosophy?
A) Fatalism
B) Humanism
C) Pragmatism
D) Secularism

3. The structure and prose style used by Steinbeck in *The Grapes of Wrath was most profoundly influenced by what work?*
A) King James Bible
B) Malory's *Morte d'Arthur*
C) Twain's *Huckleberry Finn*
D) Whitman's *Leaves of Grass*

4. The theory that human identity and self-esteem is determined by a connection to land and its cycle of growth is known as
A) Jeffersonian agrarianism
B) Neo-teological thinking
C) The concept of the Oversoul
D) The Industrial Revolution

5. What derogatory term do the citizens of California use to label the migrants?
A) Hoovies
B) Okies
C) Squatters
D) Stir-Bugs

6. What does the description of the land turtle's crossing the highway in Chapter Three symbolize?
A) Independence and the need to take risks
B) Survival and the indestructibility of the life-force
C) The futility of hard work
D) The loneliness of traveling alone

7. What social concept is best typified by Tom's statement, "I climb fences when I got fences to climb"?
A) Pragmatism
B) Romanticism
C) Socialism
D) Transcendentalism

8. Which character is often considered to be symbolic of Christ?
A) Jim Casy
B) Ma Joad
C) Rose of Sharon Joad
D) Tom Joad

9. Which Joad child makes the deliberate choice to part ways from the rest of the family?
A) Al
B) Noah
C) Rose of Sharon
D) Tom

10. Who said the following: "I'll be ever'where -- wherever you look. Wherever they's a fight so hungry people can eat, I'll be there. Wherever they's a cop beatin' up a guy, I'll be there."
A) Al Joad
B) Jim Casy
C) Muley Graves
D) Tom Joad

11. Who said the following: "There ain't no sin and there ain't no virtue. There's just stuff people do. It's all part of the same thing."
A) Jim Casy
B) Muley Graves
C) Noah Joad
D) Tom Joad

12. Who said the following: "If you're in trouble or hurt or need -- go to poor people. They're the only ones that'll help -- the only ones."
A) Jim Casy
B) Ma Joad
C) Rose of Sharon Joad
D) Sairy Wilson

13. Who said the following: ". . . if a fella's got somepin to eat an' another fella's hungry -- why, the first fella ain't got no choice."
A) Ezra Huston
B) Mr. Wainwright
C) Muley Graves
D) Pa Joad

Answers: 1.C 2.B 3.A 4.A 5.B 6.B 7.A 8.A 9.B 10.D 11.A 12.B 13.C

Full Glossary for *The Grapes of Wrath*

babbitt a soft white metal of tin, lead, copper, and antimony in various proportions, used to reduce friction as in bearings.

bandanna a large, colored handkerchief, usually with a figure or pattern.

barbarians people regarded as primitive, savage, and so on.

belligerently in a hostile or quarrelsome manner.

boil an inflamed, painful, pus-filled swelling on the skin, caused by localized infection.

bolls the roundish seed pods of a plant, especially of cotton or flax.

Bolshevicky here refers a member of the Bolshevik party, a majority faction (*Bolsheviki*) of the Russian Social Democratic Workers' Party, which formed the Communist Party after seizing power in the 1917 Revolution.

boxcars fully enclosed railroad freight cars.

carrying charges the costs associated with property ownership, as taxes, upkeep, and so on.

cat slang for Caterpillar: trademark for a tractor equipped on each side with a continuous roller belt over cogged wheels, for moving over rough or muddy ground.

cat-walk a narrow, elevated walk or platform, as one along the edge of a bridge or over the engine room of a ship.

chambray a smooth fabric of cotton, made by weaving white or unbleached threads across a colored warp: used for dresses, shirts, and so on.

Cherokee a member of a North American Indian people formerly inhabiting a large area of the south Allegheny Mountains, now in Oklahoma and North Carolina.

clout power or influence.

con-rod bearing a reciprocating rod connecting two or more moving parts of a machine, as the crankshaft and a piston of an automobile.

cord any force acting as a tie or bond.

coroner a public officer whose chief duty is to determine the causes of any deaths not obviously due to natural causes.

corrugated iron sheet iron or steel with parallel grooves and ridges to give it added strength in construction.

cottonwood a rapidly growing lowland tree.

coupe a closed, two-door automobile.

Cracker Jack trademark for a confection of sweet, glazed popcorn and peanuts.

crags steep, rugged rocks that rise above others or project from a rock mass.

croppers sharecroppers.

croquet an outdoor game in which the players use mallets to drive a wooden ball through a series of hoops placed in the ground.

cultivators implements or machines for loosening the earth and destroying weeds around growing plants.

culvert a pipe-like construction of stone, concrete, or metal, that passes under a road, railroad track, footpath, or through an embankment.

cynically in a manner that indicates a belief that people are motivated in all their actions only by selfishness.

denunciation a public accusation or strong condemnation of someone or something.

Depression the period of economic depression which began in 1929 and lasted through most of the 1930s.

diesel a type of internal-combustion engine that burns fuel oil.

disconsolately so unhappy that nothing will comfort; inconsolable; dejected.

dispossessed deprived of the possession of something, especially land, a house, and so on.

dogs slang term for feet.

drawers underpants with either short or long legs.

Dutch-oven a metal container for roasting meats, with an open side placed so that it is toward the fire.

eddied moved with a circular motion against the main current.

embalming the process of treating a dead body with various chemicals, usually after removing the viscera, to keep it from decaying rapidly.

epaulets shoulder ornaments for certain uniforms, especially military uniforms.

exhortation a plea or sermon urging or warning people to do what is required.

fallow land plowed but not seeded for one or more growing seasons, to kill weeds, make the soil richer, and so on.

feral untamed; wild.

ferment to excite; agitate.

fetid having a bad smell, as of decay.

flagged sent (a message) by signaling.

foxtails plants with cylindrical spikes bearing spikelets interspersed with stiff bristles.

freshets a sudden overflowing of a stream because of melting snow or heavy rain.

gaunt thin and bony.

gelding a castrated male horse.

Geronimo (c. 1829-1909), Apache Indian chief.

gingham a yarn-dyed cotton cloth, usually woven in stripes, checks, or plaids.

graft the act of taking advantage of one's position to gain items such as money and property dishonestly, as in politics.

hackles the hairs on a dog's neck and back that bristle, as when the dog is ready to fight.

hams a) the backs of the thighs; b) the thighs and buttocks together.

handbill a small printed notice or advertisement to be passed out by hand.

harrows frames with spikes or sharp-edged disks, drawn by a horse or tractor and used for breaking up and leveling plowed ground, covering seeds, rooting up weeds, and so on.

haycocks small, conical heaps of hay drying in a field.

head of wild oats the uppermost part of a plant's foliage.

heliograph a permanent image formed on a glass plate by an early photographic process.

hobnailed describing boots or heavy shoes with short, broad-headed nails in the soles.

Hooverville any of the encampments of displaced persons especially prevalent during the 1930's; "Hoover" is a reference to the President of the United States at the time, Herbert Hoover.

intermittent stopping and starting at intervals.

J.P. Morgan (1867-1943) U.S. financier; known as "Jack," to distinguish from his better-known father, J.P. "Pierpont" Morgan.

jack [old slang] money.

jalopy [slang] an old, ramshackle automobile.

Jefferson, Thomas (1743-1826), American statesman, third president of the United States (1801-1809), drew up the Declaration of Independence.

Jehovites members of a proselytizing Christian sect founded by Charles T. Russell (1852-1916).

jimson weed a poisonous annual weed.

kerosene lamps lamps that burn kerosene, a thin oil distilled from petroleum or shale oil.

lemon [slang] something, especially a manufactured article, that is defective or imperfect.

Lenin, Vladimir Ilyich (1870-1924), Russian leader of the Communist revolution of 1917, premier of the U.S.S.R. (1917-1924).

levee an embankment built alongside a river to prevent high water from flooding bordering land.

lifer [slang] a person sentenced to imprisonment for life.

lodge a local chapter of a fraternal organization.

lynchin' to murder (an accused person) by mob action and without lawful trial, as by hanging.

mallet a long-handled hammer with a cylindrical wooden head, used in playing croquet.

Marx, Karl (Heinrich) (1818-1883), German social philosopher and economist, in London after 1850, founder of modern socialism.

McAlester State Penitentiary near McAlester, Oklahoma.

meerschaum a soft, claylike, heat-resistant mineral used for tobacco pipes.

meetin' an assembly or place of assembly for worship.

migrant a farm laborer who moves from place to place to harvest seasonal crops.

Mother Hubbard a full loose gown for women.

muslin any of various strong, often sheer cotton cloths of plain weave; especially, a heavy variety used for sheets, pillowcases, and so on.

nestin' to place or settle; in or as in a nest.

newsreel a short motion picture of recent news events, shown as part of the program in motion picture theaters.

oat beard a hairy outgrowth on the head of certain grains and grasses.

Okie a migratory agricultural worker, forced to migrate from Oklahoma or other areas of the Great Plains because of drought and farm foreclosure in the 1930s.

"on-relief" aid in the form of goods or money given, as by a government agency, to persons unable to support themselves.

Paine, Thomas (1737-1809), American Revolutionary patriot, writer, and political theoretician, born in England.

panhandle a strip of land projecting like the handle of a pan. Here refers to the western extension of Oklahoma.

pauper any person who is extremely poor.

pellagra a chronic disease caused by a deficiency of nicotinic acid in the diet and characterized by gastrointestinal disturbances, skin eruptions, and mental disorders.

perplexity the condition of being perplexed; bewilderment; confusion.

Pilgrim's Progress a religious allegory by John Bunyan (1678).

pone cornbread in the form of small, oval loaves.

premium an additional amount paid or charged.

prodigal here refers to the wastrel son in biblical scripture who was welcomed back warmly on his homecoming in repentance (Luke 15:11-32).

proprietor one who owns and operates a business establishment.

Purty Boy Floyd infamous Depression-era bank robber; known for his kindness to poor people.

pustules small elevations of the skin containing pus.

putrescence the state or condition of something that is decomposing or rotting.

quarantine any isolation or restriction on travel or passage imposed to keep contagious diseases, insect pests, and so on from spreading.

rakishly dashingly; jauntily.

red agitators political radicals or revolutionaries, especially applied to Communists, who stir up people in support of a cause.

repel to drive or force back; hold or ward off.

salts refers here to smelling salts; an aromatic mixture, used as an inhalant in relieving faintness, headaches, and so on.

Salvation Army an international organization for religious and philanthropic purposes among the very poor.

Sam Browne belt a military officer's belt with a diagonal strap across the right shoulder, designed to carry the weight of a pistol or sword.

self-abasement a humbling or abasement of oneself.

serfs persons in feudal servitude, bound to a master's land and transferred with it to a new owner.

service clubs clubs, such as Rotary and Kiwanis, organized to provide certain services for their members and to promote the community welfare.

servile humbly yielding or submissive.

shim a thin, usually wedge-shaped piece of wood, metal, or stone used for filling space, leveling, and so on, as in masonry.

shirtwaist a woman's blouse or bodice tailored more or less like a shirt.

shuck to remove a shell, pod, or husk.

side-meat meat from the side of a pig; specifically, bacon or salt pork.

sidled moved sideways, especially in a shy or stealthy manner.

signet ring a finger ring containing a seal, often in the form of an initial or monogram.

single-action Colt a type of revolver invented by American Samuel Colt (1814-1862) — the hammer must be cocked by hand before each shot.

singletree a wooden bar swung at the center from a hitch on a plow, wagon, and so on, and hooked at either end to the traces of a horse's harness.

skitters slang term for diarrhea.

spam trademark for a kind of canned luncheon meat made from pieces of seasoned pork and ham pressed into a loaf.

speaking in tongues ecstatic or apparently ecstatic utterance of usually unintelligible speechlike sounds, as in a religious assembly, viewed by some as a manifestation of deep religious experience.

squatters persons who settle on public or unoccupied land.

St. Louis Fair the World's Fair of 1900 held in St. Louis, Missouri. The World's Fair is an exposition at which arts, crafts, industrial, and agricultural products of various countries of the world are on display.

stereopticon a kind of slide projector designed to allow one view to fade out while the next is fading in.

stir-bugs [slang] prison inmates.

straw bosses supervisors who have little or no authority to support their orders.

strike a concerted refusal by employees to go on working in an attempt to force an employer to grant certain demands, as for higher wages, better working conditions, and so on.

strikebreaking the act of one who attempts to break up a strike, often by intimidating striking workers.

syphilis an infectious venereal disease usually transmitted by sexual intercourse or acquired congenitally.

tappet a sliding rod in an engine or machine moved by intermittent contact with a cam and used to move another part, as a valve.

tarpaulin a waterproof sheet spread over something to protect it from getting wet.

Tehachapi mountain just east of Bakersfield.

tenant a person who farms land owned by another and pays rent in cash or in a share of the crops.

to act flip [colloq.] to act flippantly or impertinently.

touring car an early type of open automobile, often with a folding top, seating five or more passengers.

truck skinner a skinner is a mule driver; here refers to a truck driver.

tunics short coats worn by soldiers, policemen, and so on.

two bits [informal] 25 cents.

two-by-four any length of lumber two inches thick and four inches wide when untrimmed.

union something united or unified; a whole made up of parts; esp. an organization or confederation uniting various individuals, political units, and so on.

vagrant one who wanders from place to place without a regular job, supporting oneself by begging.

vigilantes members of vigilance committees, groups that keep order or punish crime without legal authority.

win'fall peaches here refers to windfall peaches; something blown down by the wind, as fruit from a tree.

Essay Questions

1. What is the purpose of the intercalary chapters? (See essay on structure and refer to commentaries following each intercalary chapter.)

2. How does the economic decline of the Joad family correspond to the disintegration of their family?

3. Describe Tom's spiritual journey from inner, intuitive morality to an outward expression of morality that encompasses all of humanity.

4. Describe briefly the social and historical background in which *The Grapes of Wrath* was created. How did this affect the novel's public and critical reception? How has this reception changed as the historical events that shaped the novel have receded into the distant past?

5. Explain the symbolism of the turtle in Chapter 3.

Practice Projects

1. Examine the intercalary chapters to find passages which seem to reflect some of Steinbeck's philosophies. Compare these passages with dialogue delivered by the novel's main characters to determine to what extent Steinbeck's perspective is similar or different.

2. Compare Steinbeck's journalistic accounts of the migrant story found in newspaper articles from *The San Francisco News* and the pamphlet "Their Blood Was Strong" to his account of the migrant workers in *The Grapes of Wrath*. Based on Steinbeck's use of the two mediums to tell the same story, draw some conclusions on the differences between fiction and journalism.

3. Describe briefly the social and historical background in which *The Grapes of Wrath* was created. How did this context affect the novel's public and critical reception? How has this reception changed as the historical events that shaped the novel have receded into the distant past?

4. How has the condition of the migrant farm workers changed since *The Grapes of Wrath* was first published in 1939? Did the novel have any influence, direct or indirect, in the changes that have occurred?

NOTES

NOTES

CPSIA information can be obtained
at www.ICGtesting.com
Printed in the USA
BVHW052249090223
658263BV00007B/285